The SPELIT Power Matrix

Copyright © 2007 June Schmieder-Ramirez Ph.D. and Leo A.
Mallette Ed.D., Editors
All rights reserved.
ISBN: 1-4196-7191-X
ISBN-13: 978-1419671913

Visit www.booksurge.com to order additional copies.

The SPELIT Power Matrix
Untangling the Organizational Environment With the SPELIT Leadership Tool

June Schmieder-Ramirez Ph.D.
Leo A. Mallette Ed.D.,
Editors

2007

The SPELIT Power Matrix

Table of Contents

Introduction ix
Editors' Acknowledgments xiii
Author Biographies xvii

    Part I. Why SPELIT?. 1
1. The Theoretical Foundations of SPELIT. 3
2. Integrating Adult Learning and the SPELIT
    Analysis Methodology 13

    Part II. The SPELIT Environments. 25
3. The SPELIT Model 27
4. On the Social Aspects of Organization:
    "The Human Side of Enterprise" Revisited 33
5. Political Environment 55
6. Assessment of the Economic Environment 63
7. Assessing the Legal Environment. 73
8. Analyzing the Intercultural Dynamics Within an
    Organization 91
9. The Technology Component of the SPELIT
    Environmental Analysis Model. 107
10. Environmental Epilogue 129

    Part III. Applications 135
11. Applications, Formats & Examples. 137
12. An Organizational Example 149
    Final Conclusions 159

Introduction
Dr. Leo A. Mallette, Editor

The SPELIT POWER MATRIX analysis methodology was developed for students to have a framework for determining and formulating the answer to the question: What is? This methodology is intended for practitioners doing a market analysis or diagnosis prior to implementing transitions or benchmarking in anticipation of an intervention. This methodology can be used by undergraduate students and seasoned practitioners. This book will show how this methodology aligns with established and more current theories and will delineate a new environmental analysis technique that is used to systematically analyze the social, political, economic, legal, intercultural, and technological aspects of an environment. Portions of this book were originally described in Schmieder-Ramirez and Mallette (2006).

One problem is that many authors of change theories stipulate benchmarking or diagnosing the current condition as a first step in the change process (Christiansen, 1997; Cummings & Worley, 2005; Holcomb, 2001; Kaufman, 2000). This first step may be specific as in Holcomb's book *Asking the Right Questions*. Her first question is "Where are we now?" (p. 17).This first step can also be implied as in Lewin (1951), who has a three step process for implementing a transition. His first step, *unfreezing,* requires being able to show differences between the existing condition of the organization and to understand what is being unfrozen (and by how much). This requires knowledge of the organization in its current environment.This book adds a new tool to your toolbox of organization analysis instruments. You will learn several methods that are variations of the SPELIT methodology. Specialists in the areas of organizational leadership, law, and sociology will describe the elements of SPELIT and provide a multi-disciplinary tool to evaluate the environment of an organization. Just like any tool (such as a hammer), you don't have to use all functions of the tool. You can use a claw hammer to pull nails all day long, without ever driving a nail. You can also use it to drive nails. It can also be used with other tools such as a center punch to create a dimple in a piece of metal to align the point of a drill bit. Similarly, the various environments of SPELIT can be used or not used. You can even add your own environments. SPELIT can also be used with other tools like fishbone diagrams and Pareto plots.

There is a need to analyze the environment in all aspects of life. People perform an environmental analysis when contemplating a new job, a different house, or a marriage (or at least they *should* do so). It is always beneficial to enter a new organization knowing what you are getting into! Mathematicians call the existing environment when they look at a problem, the *initial conditions* or *initial state*. SPELIT helps define the initial state of your organization. Nehemiah, around 450 BCE (Before Common Era), circled the city and performed an evaluation of the walls and gates of Jerusalem as part of his wall reconstruction project management task, albeit by moonlight (Nehemiah, chapter 2, verse 13). There are many works comparable to SPELIT. Most change theories have a chapter dedicated to existing conditions or diagnosing the current condition.

In the article *Environmental Scanning: Radar for Success,* Albright (2004) defines environmental scanning as "a method for identifying, collecting, and translating information about external influences into useful plans and decisions" (p. 40). She presents this in a summary article on environmental scanning and references several excellent articles and texts dating back to 1967. Her definition of environmental scanning differs from SPELIT in that environmental scanning addresses external influences and translates them into plans, while SPELIT is used to create a baseline of both internal and external environments and does not prepare plans for change. Both methods consider some of the same topics because several of Albright's environments are the same as the SPELIT environments. Similarly, Thompson, Strickland, and Gamble's (2005) book on *Crafting and Executing Strategy* discusses analyzing the company. They present the need to analyze "a company's external environment" (pp. 44-85) including the macroenvironment. Their macroenvironment contains several of the elements of SPELIT, but is applied to the environment external to the company. For the internal mechanics of a company—such as a division, a department, or even one person working in the organization—you may need to consider the SPELIT environments in which you are working.

There are other ways of viewing the SPELIT environments. One of them is *reframing*. To do any reframing of our views of an organization, we need to understand where we are. Bolman and Deal (2003) identify four frames of reference: 1) structural, 2) human resource, 3) political, and 4) symbolic (p. 16). Each of these frames is a point of view and can be useful for evaluating the environment of an organization. These four frames are incorporated into several categories of the SPELIT analysis model. Bygrave and Zacharakis (2004) identified the *Five Cs* framework for systematically analyzing an organization: context, customers, competitors, collaborators, and company (pp. 73-75). A key step in the *general model of planned change* is diagnosis (Cummings & Worley, 2005, pp. 28-30). The authors discuss diagnosing organizations, diagnosing groups within organizations, and diagnosing individuals prior to designing interventions. To this list we would add diagnosing the environment outside of the organization.

***

Overview of This Book

This book presents the SPELIT POWER MATRIX analysis methodology in three parts. There is a one-page introduction to each part of the book.

Part I discusses theory (Chapter 1) and the importance to adult learning (Chapter 2). Part II describes the SPELIT model (Chapter 3) and a detailed discussion of each environment (Chapters 4 to 10). The third part of this book presents examples, formats, and applications and summary conclusions (Chapters 11 and 12). The names of the organizations have been changed to provide anonymity. The external authoritative industry information that was used for this analysis was properly referenced without directly quoting the actual firm.

***

References

Albright, K. S. (2004). Environmental scanning: Radar for success. *Information Management Journal, 38*(3), 38-45.

Bolman, L., & Deal, T. (2003). *Reframing organizations, Artistry, choice, and leadership*. San Francisco CA: Jossey-Bass.

Bygrave, W., & Zacharakis, A. (2004). *The portable MBA in entrepreneurship* (3rd ed.). Hoboken, NJ: John Wiley & Sons.

Christiansen, C. M. (1997). Making strategy: Learning by doing. *Harvard Business Review*, 3-12.

Cummings, T., & Worley, C. (2005). *Organization development & change* (8th ed.). Mason, OH: South-Western.

Holcomb, E. (2001). *Asking the right questions: Techniques for collaboration and school change.* Thousand Oaks CA: Corwin Press.

Kaufman, J. (2000). *Mega planning: Practical tools for organizational success.* Thousand Oaks CA: Sage.

Schmieder-Ramirez, J., & Mallette, L. (2006). *An introduction to the SPELIT© interdisciplinary analysis methodology.* Paper presented at the Society of Educators and Scholars Conference, Long Beach CA.

Thompson, A., Strickland, A., & Gamble, J. (2005). *Crafting and executing strategy: The quest for competitive advantage* (14th ed.). New York: McGraw-Hill.

Editors' Acknowledgments
From June Schmieder-Ramirez, Ph.D.

I am grateful for the tremendous support I have received in the production of what we feel will be an important book. I must thank my professors at Stanford University for providing me with the thoughts, academic perspectives, and insights to enable me to edit this text. They provided our classes with books such as Graham Allison's *Essence of Decision*, which opened up a new vista of how to analyze complex situations. They provided challenging problems for us to debate. They encouraged us to think about how the culture that surrounds us is a key in making good decisions.

I would also like to thank Pepperdine University for its support of my research over the past 15 years. The university has provided a lighthouse to me due to its strong sense of mission.

I would also like to thank the Organizational Leadership doctoral students at Pepperdine University for critical reviews of the evaluation copy of this book. Dr. Farzin Madjidi is the program director of this program and Ms. Christie Dailo is the program administrator. Without the support of the students in this program, this book would not be completed.

In addition I would like to thank my son, Dr. David Marr, professor at the Colorado School of Mines, for his insight into how to analyze complex organizations. I would like to thank my husband Ramon Ramirez who keeps me grounded in reality.

Furthermore, I would like to thank the authors who stepped forward to help us write this text. They each have a particular skill that provided a perfect fit with their authorship. They took time out of their busy schedules to help produce this book.

Finally, I would like to thank my co-editor Dr. Leo A. Mallette. He is the person who took a model I had been using for years, expanded it, and forged an idea of how SPELIT could be used to analyze complex organizations. His skills as an editor and "organizer" are unparalleled. Without the help and encouragement of those noted above, this book could not have been written.

June Schmieder-Ramirez, Ph.D.
June 2007

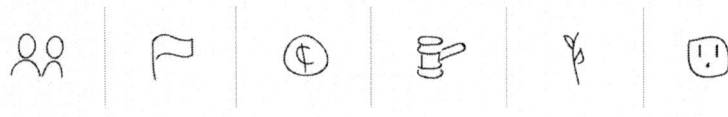

Figure. The SPELIT Environments. Design by Margaret Minnis Design (minnisdesign.com).

From Leo A. Mallette, Ed.D.

I too would like to acknowledge the chapter, section, and artwork contributors. Without them, this book would be an empty notebook with a boring cover! Their biographies are listed on the next few pages in alphabetical order. They are experts in their fields. By contributing to this book, they are giving back to society and to their fields of expertise. Their biographies are extensive, varied, and interesting. They are all professionals that I have been delighted to know.

Pepperdine University has a special place in my soul. I am a better person because of the people there, the professors, administrators, and students. I was especially motivated, at the beginning of my doctoral studies, by a comment from Dr. Farzin Madjidi. He asked if this was going to be a $70,000 doctorate (the cost of the classes) or a million dollar doctorate? He was implying that, like many things in life, you get more out of what you put more into. That prompted me and several of my peers to do more. This book started when I was finishing my dissertation, and was probably one extra project that I didn't need. But I really enjoyed *doing* this book.

Special thanks goes to my co-editor Professor June Schmieder-Ramirez for relighting the publishing fire within me, and during a casual conversation mentioning, "You should write a book." So I did. Fellow doctoral students Leslie Evans, Clare Berger, and I started writing a book (http://www.writingforconferences.com/). That book is in progress, and this one is done. Thanks June!

Finally, I'd like to thank the most important person in my life: my beautiful wife Kathy. Not only has she spent most evenings of the last several years watching me disappear into the dissertation cave, she has had to endure more months while I was preparing this manuscript. But the effort on the dissertation and this book finally abated, and the house remodel was started. That's turning out to be another book! Thank you again Kathy.

Leo A. Mallette, Ed.D.
June 2007

Figure. The SPELIT Environments. Design by Margaret Minnis Design (minnisdesign.com).

Author Biographies
(In Alphabetical Order by Last Name)

Eugene Anton (Section Author) is a doctoral student in Organizational Leadership at Pepperdine University, California. Mr. Anton holds an M.B.A. with concentrations in Finance and International Business, a B.A. in Business Administration, and a B.S. in Finance. He has developed expertise while managing organizations that are in need of or experiencing significant organizational change. Mr. Anton has focused his attentions on the family business system and entrepreneurial ventures.

Jim DellaNeve (Section Author) is a doctoral candidate in Organizational Leadership at Pepperdine University. Jim holds a B.S. in Business Management from Pepperdine University and an MBA from the Claremont Graduate School. He has 20 years of experience in the aerospace industry in various areas related to engineering design, engineering and manufacturing information systems, product development processes, and strategy formulation and planning. Jim has a passion for large scale organizational learning and its relationship to organizational change.

MD Haque (Chapter Author) is a doctoral student in Organizational Leadership at the Graduate School of Education and Psychology at Pepperdine University. Mr. Haque has strong analytical and technological skills through extensive work experience. Mr. Haque has a Bachelors Degree in Public Administration and three Masters Degrees in Public Administration, Business Administration, and Business Technologies. He has presented in various refereed academic conferences and published in conference proceedings including Hawaii International Conference on Education (2006), International Academy of Business and Public Administration Disciplines (IABPAD) Conference (2006), and the Society of Educators and Scholars Conference (2006). He has also been accepted to present in the Organizational Development Network Conference in San Francisco in October 2006.

Dr. Michael Lacourse (Chapter Author, mlacours@csulb.edu) is currently Associate Dean of the College of Health and Human Services and Professor of Kinesiology at California State University, Long Beach. His doctoral training is in Motor Learning and Educational Inquiry Methodology. He has been a faculty member, Coordinator of Graduate Programs in Kinesiology, Chair of the Department of Kinesiology, and Director of the Neuromotor Rehabilitation Research Laboratory at the Veteran's Affairs Medical Center in Long Beach over the past 18 years. His research is aimed at evaluating functional brain reorganization subsequent to spinal cord injury and testing therapeutic interventions targeted at stimulating brain plasticity for motor recovery. He has over 40 peer-reviewed published articles and abstracts and has made over 50 presentations at scholarly meetings.

Dr. Mark Maier (Chapter Author) is Associate Professor of Sociology and Founding Chair of the leadership programs at Chapman University in Orange, California, where he also directs the Chapman Leadership Project. The recipient of the 1999 Distinguished Educator Award from the Organizational Behavior Teaching Society, Dr. Maier is recognized as one of the most outstanding teachers in his discipline in the country. He lectures and consults widely in the areas of servant-leadership, communication, team development, and ethics. Together with his wife, Lori Zucchino, he has developed and facilitated extensive leadership development programs for such organizations as the Internal Revenue Service, the County of Orange, the City of Anaheim, and the City of Palm Desert. He has received numerous academic awards for both his teaching and his scholarship, has consulted with NBC News, PBS, the Discovery Channel, MS/NBC, the BBC, and been cited in many national publications. He obtained his Ph.D. in Social Organization and Social Change from Cornell University in 1986, with minors in Industrial and Labor Relations and Educational Psychology.

Dr. Leo A. Mallette (Editor and Chapter Author, leokathy96@aol.com) has worked in the aerospace industry since 1974 and is currently managing high technology contracts. He received the BSE and MSE degrees in electrical engineering from the University of Central Florida and the MBA and Ed.D degrees from Pepperdine University. He has published over 50 conference and journal articles on atomic frequency standards, satellite systems, ground stations, optical detectors, circuits, genealogy, and organizational leadership. Dr. Mallette is a senior member of the Institute of Electrical and Electronics Engineers, a member of the advisory board for the Precise Time and Time Interval Conference, and a board member of the Society of Educators and Scholars. He and his wife Kathy live in Irvine and Rancho Mirage, California.

Elizabeth Martin (Chapter Author, Emartin@csulb.edu) is a doctoral student in Organizational Leadership at Pepperdine University. Irvine, California. She has an M.A. in Public Administration and a B.A., in English from California State University, Long Beach, California. Elizabeth has extensive experience in finance, budget, human resources and management, training, and compensation. She has held several management positions prior to her position as the Administrative Services Manager at California State University, Long Beach. In addition, she is also an adjunct faculty member and teaches leadership and professional writing in the Graduate Center for Public Policy and Administration at CSULB.

Gale R. Mazur (Chapter Author, GRMazur@pepperdine.edu) is a Senior Consultant specializing in strategic human resource management, organizational effectiveness, training, and leadership development. A certified administrator of the Intercultural Development Inventory, she works with profit and non-profit organizations to identify and address issues caused by diversity in the workplaces. Mazur teaches organizational behavior, leadership, and critical thinking at Chapman University and facilitates classes frequently online in the University of Phoenix's business and management program. A doctoral candidate studying organizational leadership at Pepperdine University, she has co-authored a variety of articles including "The Benefits of an International Experience," "Team Leadership," and "21st Century Leadership and its Intersection with Organizational Culture." Married with two children, including a son adopted from Honduras, she holds a Master of Arts in Human Resource Development from George Washington University, Washington, D.C.

Margaret Minnis (Artist, www.minnisdesign.com) is an award-winning graphic artist who specializes in corporate brand identity initiatives, creative development, logo creation, web page design, direct mailings, and advertising programs. Minnis is a member of the board of directors of the Orange County, California chapter of the American Institute of Graphic Arts. She holds a Bachelor of Fine Arts in Graphic Design from Chapman University.

Michael A. Moodian (Chapter Author, http://www.moodian.com) is a cross-cultural management consultant, an adjunct faculty member at Chapman and Vanguard universities and a doctoral candidate studying organizational leadership at Pepperdine University. His first book, *Contemporary Leadership and Intercultural Competence: Understanding and*

Utilizing Cultural Diversity to Build Successful Organizations, will be released worldwide in 2008. Moodian's memberships include the International Academy for Intercultural Research and the Society for Human Resource Management. He holds a Master of Arts, Communications from California State University, Fullerton.

Jacqueline B. Pritchett (Chapter Author) is a doctoral student at Pepperdine University studying for her Ed.D. in Organizational Leadership. She has a master's degree in Adult Education and Human Resource Development from Fordham University in New York City. She has effectively developed and conducted workshops for adult learners. Jacqueline has diverse interests, which include adult learning, women, and youth leadership, curriculum development, cultural diversity training, workplace development, research, traveling, volunteering, writing, and classic photography. She is a published author of poetry. She is also a book reviewer for the adult education journal *Perspectives*. Jacqueline is a member of the Phi Kappa Phi Academic Honor Society and a Bill Gates Millennium Scholar.

Mark Romejko (Section Author) is a doctoral candidate in Organizational Leadership at Pepperdine University. Mr. Romejko holds a B.S. in Business Administration from the University of Redlands and an MBA from Pepperdine University. He has over 30 years of experience in the government sector primarily in the areas of finance, resource administration, human resources, and contracts. His current research is focused on leadership succession planning in government research organizations. Mr. Romejko enjoys writing and assisting non-profit organizations.

Dr. June Schmieder-Ramirez (Editor and Chapter Author) is the Interim Associate Dean/Professor of Education at Pepperdine University. She has co-authored five books on educational administration and one text on higher education assessment *The Accreditors are Coming*. She has published over 30 articles on leadership. Her research interests include experiential education, school finance, and school personnel. She has one son, David M. Marr, who is a professor at the School of Mines in Golden Colorado. She resides in Quail Valley California with her husband, Ramon. She is currently working on a book on experiential learning for student teachers and medical interns with Jack McManus, a colleague at Pepperdine.

Dr. Maurice M. Shihadi, Ed.D. (Chapter Author, maurice@adjuncts.net) earned his doctorate in Organizational Leadership at Pepperdine University. His current research interests concern service quality assessment in technology based organizations. He received his M.S.in Occupational Studies from the California State University, Long Beach School of Human Resources with an emphasis in administration. Dr.

Shihadi has worked as a small business technical writer, consultant, and adjunct professor of business and computer applications since 1986. He is currently founder and CEO of Anacru.com and Adjuncts.net. Anacru.com is a Rockville-based small face-to-face business management consultancy with an emphasis on technology integration, applications training, and financial planning. Adjuncts.net is a start-up web based consultancy that provides free email and email forwarding to adjunct professors in addition to a variety of other paid services including web hosting, technical writing, post production audio, and web course management technical support services. Maurice currently lives in Silver Spring, Maryland.

Dr. David Silverberg (Section Author) is an Assistant Professor at the Schar College of Education at Ashland University. Dr. Silverberg holds an Ed.D. and an M.S. from Pepperdine University and a B.A. from Wesleyan University. His 17 years in education include teaching, administering, consulting, researching, and writing. He has presented at conferences in Italy, Switzerland, and throughout the United States. He is the Associate Managing Editor for the *Scholar & Educator*. His expanding research of Character Education welcomes novel programs for assessment and documentation. Dr. Silverberg resides Ohio, the birthplace of aviation and bipolar voting.

John Tobin, J.D. (Chapter Author) is an adjunct professor who holds dual appointments in Pepperdine University's Graduate Schools of Education and Psychology and in Business and Management. He has lectured on business law, negotiation theory, bankruptcy law, and legal research and writing, at Pepperdine University, at the University of La Verne, and the University of California, Riverside, beginning in 1995. When not at the lectern, Professor Tobin is a United States Administrative Law Judge. When not on the bench, Judge Tobin is a Colonel in the Judge Advocate General's Corps of the U.S. Army Reserve. He is a 1981 graduate of the Judge Advocate General's School at the University of Virginia; a 1980 Juris Doctor graduate of the University of Louisville, School of Law; and a 1974 Honor's Program graduate B.A. at the University of Kentucky in 1974. He was designated as a Mediator for the Bankruptcy Court of the Central District of California and the Superior Court, Riverside County California in 1995.

Joseph Yu (Chapter Author) has a strong analytical knowledge and functional management knowledge in business management processes. He is skilled in forecasting, managing, and reporting of indirect resources, budgets, manpower, capital projects, training, space facilities, and six sigma projects. He has a strong technical expertise in electronic systems design and system integration in the area of airborne radar electronics as an engineering supervisor. Mr. Yu is Pursuing a

Doctorate in Organizational Leadership at Pepperdine University. He has earned an MBA, an M.S. and a B.S. in Electrical Engineering. Mr. Yu presented at Hawaii International Conference on Education (2006) on global leadership and intercultural learning, which was published in the conference proceedings. He also presented at the International Academy of Business and Public Administration Disciplines Conference and Society of Educators and Scholars Conference in 2006.

Part I
Why SPELIT?

The idea of the **SPELIT POWER MATRIX** is rooted in many disciplines and is brought together by a desire to lead people and manage organizations. The two chapters in this section provide a background to some of the theorists that have influenced this field and have studied how we learn.

The purpose of the first chapter is to present the theory behind the major sections of the SPELIT model. Each of the assumptions of the framework are addressed by Dr. Schmieder-Ramirez and the chapter introduces the thinking that served as a foundational value to that part of the model. We must know ourselves as well as our environment before we can be effective in leadership, and SPELIT can be used to assess our own strengths and to assess the individual's organization.

In the second chapter, Jacqueline B. Pritchett provides a peek at the world of adult learning and why this is important to us. As adult learners, we must equip ourselves with methods that will assist in our decision-making process throughout our personal lives, professions, and academic careers. We must think critically about inevitable influences that will determine a successful presence in today's domestic and global marketplaces.

This part of the book answers the questions of *who* are the theorists that drive the **SPELIT** method and *why* do we, as adult learners, want to learn.

Chapter 1
The Theoretical Foundations of SPELIT

Dr. June Schmieder-Ramirez
Pepperdine University

Knowing others is intelligence; knowing yourself is true wisdom; mastering others is strength; mastering yourself is true wisdom.

Sun Tzu

***

Introduction

The SPELIT POWER MATRIX methodology, which has been instrumental in revitalizing the thinking of planned change, will be introduced in this text. It was developed by Drs. June Schmieder-Ramirez and Leo Mallette and has evolved from the works of many authors. The thinking behind the theory has origins in *The Prince* by Machiavelli, in Sun Tzu, and in many theorists who believe that before a leader brings a plan to the table, it is necessary to analyze the environment very carefully. Sun Tzu in *The Art of War* stated:

> For this reason, one who does not know the plans of the feudal lords cannot forge preparatory alliances. One who does not know the topography of mountains and forests, ravines and defiles, wetlands and marshes cannot maneuver the army. One who does not employ local guides will not secure advantages of terrain. One who does not know one of these four or five cannot command the army of a hegemon or a true king. (p. 223)

SPELIT is a framework that emphasizes that it is necessary to know oneself from a social, political, economic, legal, intercultural, and technical view and the organization. The purpose of this chapter is to present the theory behind the major sections of the SPELIT model. Each of the assumptions of the framework will be addressed in turn as to the thinking that served as a foundational value to that part of the model. In addition, the importance of the driving and restraining forces will be addressed. After all the portions of the model are presented, then selected applications will be noted in the summary and conclusions of this chapter, although the conclusion chapter of this book will address these issues also.

***

Why was SPELIT Developed?

It is well known that you must know yourself as well as your environment before you can be effective in leadership. SPELIT can be used to assess your own strengths and to assess the individual's organization. In contrast to a SWOT (strengths, weaknesses, opportunities, and threats) analysis SPELIT takes a laser beam and analyzes the individual in the context of the organization. In a SWOT analysis, the assessment is fairly rote and does not take into consideration human strengths and weaknesses as much as SPELIT.

Who might use SPELIT? Those who might use this tool include anyone who needs to analyze an organization, assess yourself, and move forward with plans. Since we encounter change every day of our lives we can use this model consciously and unconsciously to assess where we are. Those who might use SPELIT are student teachers, architect apprentices, state department employees, strategic planners, construction foremen, doctoral students, professors, and anyone who needs to constantly assess the environment for changes.

***

Why are Theoretical Frameworks Important?

Theoretical frameworks are important because they help us to organize our thoughts. For example, Graham Allison's *Essence of Decision* is an excellent text because it uses the rational, political, and organizational frames to analyze the Cuban Missile crisis. The complexities of this major event are better understood using this model. For the rational part of the model, the thinking of both the United States' political advisors and the Russian advisors were analyzed. For the political part of the analysis, the incident was analyzed according to the groups involved and the implications of their decisions. For the organizational analysis, the bureaucracies of the Soviet Union and the United States were analyzed to determine what the responses of both nations would be.

Another example of a model to assess organizations is Bolman and Deal's *Reframing organizations*. In this text the organization is assessed according to the structural and human resources frames of reference.

What are Driving Forces?

Kurt Lewin discussed the importance of driving forces in his text: *Resolving Social Conflicts and Field Theory in Social Science,* (1997). He also produced work in 1947 that speaks to the human dynamics of behavior. He notes that there are driving forces in many human actions. Lewin was interested in conceptualizing the change process in human systems. Edgar Schein from the MIT Sloan School of Management observed the significance of Lewin's Change model of *unfreeze* movement and *refreeze* as central to most change activities in organizations (Lewin, 1951). For change to occur, some kind of fundamental disequilibrium was necessary that would alter the force field (Schein, 1968). The change had to occur in the driving or restraining forces. This is why the driving forces were incorporated into the second stage of the SPELIT model. Once the model is set, then you could use the model to view the organization, and then set both driving and restraining forces in motion. Both Schein and Lewin recognized the power of culture and equilibrium in maintaining the structure of an organization.

Peter Senge (1990) notes that in any kind of learning, some kind of disequilibrium takes place before a desired outcome occurs. There should be anxiety that our survival depends on analyzing the organization and creating a new plan for ourselves. We connect the analysis that we do to some kind of information that we already possess. Lewin helped to establish new norms by involving those that would be affected by the change. There has to be a safety net that ameliorates the psychological feelings of loss before change can occur. The SPELIT model enables the individual not only to scan the present. Schein also recommends that rather than teaching any concept of change, it is important to have students actually move through a change process utilizing a project they are working on.

The process identified in this text identifies a scanning technique and then an identification of restraining and driving forces to address this scanning picture. This is an intervention and should be taken with care. Acquiring data is intrusive and working with teams to identify the driving and restraining forces is also intrusive. You must proceed with this model with all due respect and care for all those participating. What follows is a closer look at each part of the SPELIT model, delineating the theories behind each of the constructs (Figure 1-1). You will see these theories reiterated throughout this text. They are part of a cohesive way of scanning your horizon and knowing who you are before going forward in any change effort.

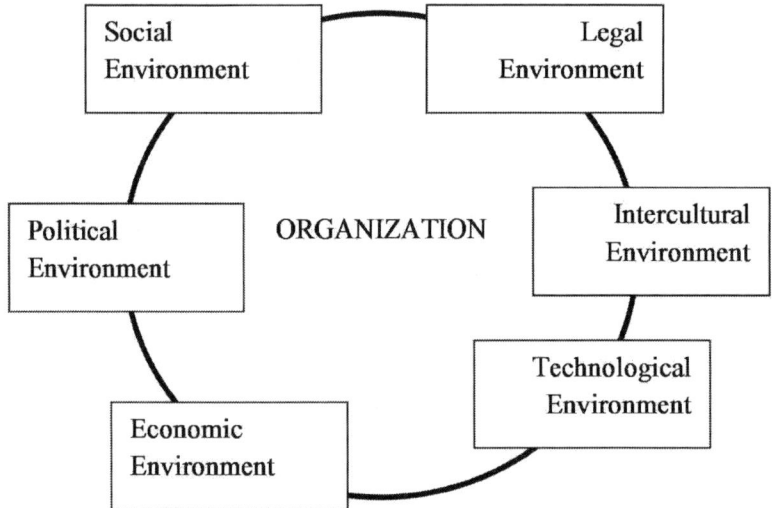

Figure 1-1. The SPELIT Model, Showing Analysis of the Environment from Outside and Within the Organization.

> *Appear at points which the enemy must hasten to defend; march swiftly to places where you are not expected.*
> *Force him to reveal himself, so as to find out his vulnerable points.*
> *He who can modify his tactics in relation to his opponent and thereby succeed in winning, may be called a "Heaven-born captain."*
>
> Sun Tzu

The Environmental Social Analysis Theoretical Framework

A definition for the social part of the framework is the assumption that it is important to assess social networks, reporting structures, and social cultural norms in an organization.

Etienne Wenger (1998) asserted in *Communities of Practice* that we should make the assumption that learning is fundamentally a deeply social activity and that it is part of our lived experience.

If we assume that this is true, we would see the organization as deeply social in nature. We would also see this social part of the organization as important in our model because everyone in the organization is connected to each other. We would assume that the process that would help us understand the social nature of the organization would include issues such as how do employees socialize and eat together at work?

How do employees remain motivated through difficult circumstances? What are the boundaries of groups that are working together? Do the boundaries become flexible like a paramecium (a single cell animal) and change with the task? Can employees move from one constellation of workers to another? How does geographical location of the employees support common tasks? How simple is it for employees to form new working communities? Do employees work from home or telecommute? These are all questions to ask when one is assessing the social graphic of an organization.

Donald A. Schon (1983) in *The Reflective Practitioner* discusses the architectural design studio as an example of "reflects-in-action" which is a social way of learning. The architectural studio is a social setting. Usually the lead architect critiques his work of the apprentices.

There are other examples where understanding the social nature of the organization and organizational learning would be beneficial. In many organizations it is important to set up research groups where individuals work together to design new products. What are the social dimensions of these work groups? How are they structured to allow for creativity?

Thus the social section of the SPELIT model emphasizes all the connectedness that makes up the social community of the organization. You should observe how community is celebrated, task groups are organized, and shared interests are maintained. This is a crucial portion of the SPELIT model and one which indicates how the culture is configured in a very tangible way.

Political Environment Analysis Section

The political analysis framework can be viewed as how an organization deals with competing interests, views, assumptions, and values. Our society does accommodate many different political viewpoints, but occasionally there are *shifts in the tectonic plates* that set off major debate. For example in today's newspaper there are articles regarding the debate between supporting American made automobiles or purchasing Asian brands. It is important to gather all information about this debate as many Asian based companies hire American workers. However, this is a political debate that is ongoing.

In order to understand the foundation of political thought, it is necessary to read the political thoughts of Rawls, Kant, Rousseau, Aristotle, and Plato. All have their strong views on the nature of man and the political state. The rise of political thought can be traced to over 6000 B.C. with the rise of the city-states and the formation of craftsmen and guilds. This is the time of the beginning of the social strata which we have today. However, to analyze a modern organization, you should not only look at the organization chart but look at who has access to resources within the organization. The reporting arrangements are also important. The questions of power, including *legitimate power* (the power of authority), *referent power* (those who are close to persons of authority), *expert power* (leading from experience or education), and *incentive* or *coercive power*, are also important to assess.

In order to understand about the political inner workings of an organization, you might read Hirschhorn's (1993) text, *the Psychodynamics of Organizations*. In the text various firms are analyzed, including a law firm, to observe the dynamics of social and political activity.

Economic Environment Analysis of the Organization

How do you assess where an organization is economically? What internal and external sources are available to take a snapshot in time of what is happening?

One of the ways is to analyze a financial report, but these are not always available. Another method is to analyze a company's annual report, but this is not always available—especially for private companies. It takes some sleuthing to determine what the financial status of a company is, but it can be done. Look at what happened with Enron, as the officers of the company were encouraging the employees to purchase stock while the company was in disarray.

One way to start with a financial analysis is to sift through what resources there are, including web sites, newspaper articles, and outside analyses. The stock prices of public companies are available, and this is one place to start. An example from Harvard Business School Studies includes the Christensen Butterfield Fabric Company.

Clayton Christensen (1997), in *Making Strategy by Doing*, analyzes the Butterfield Fabric Company. He found that the fabric company kept producing the same products even though its product sales were declining due to more nimble competitors. It had economies of scale, scope, and reputation, but it did not have the *right* products for the present consumer demand.

What are those economic resources that could be categorized as *human capital*? What is the educational background of those who work in that organization?

Legal Environment Analysis of the Organization

A legal analysis of the organization is vital to understanding how procedures are governed and how policies are made. Many legal policies can be found on the company website. However, you can also review what law cases have involved any litigation by organization employees. Legal drivers can also be triggered by state and federal agencies. For example, changes in the Environmental Protection Act can trigger changes at the local level.

Any organized system within an organization owes much of its existence to Thomas Hobbes who developed the social contract theory. An agreement is made among rational, equal, and *free* persons. He sought to find rational principles that would serve the public rather than move to a system of *political disintegration*.

Intercultural Environment Analysis in SPELIT

The ability to respond to cultural differences is key to being an effective global leader in this environment. The theories that support assessing the organizational environment for sensitivity in these areas were developed and are being developed by Gert Hofstede (1980), Mitch Hammer (1999), and M. J. Bennett (2004).

Many are familiar with the work of Hofstede (1980), who surveyed 116,000 IBM employees from 40 different countries to assess their orientations to cultural issues on various value dimensions. Theories that support the work in this area arise out of those in intercultural competence (IC) and intercultural sensitivity (IS). The model used to support this area is the Developmental Model of Intercultural Sensitivity (Bennett). This helps us to illustrate how a person's sensitivity to other cultures can move from a simple to complicated state. The DMIS is built upon prior theories and presents advancement in thinking in this area. There has been a long interest among trainers to find an instrument that can be used to measure those attributes associated with cultural sensitivity. The model bases its assumptions on the premise that as your ability to respond to cultural differences becomes more complex, your worldview and ways of relating to differences in others becomes more sophisticated (Bennett, J. & Bennett, M. 2004).

The IDI Inventory is divided into six stages: denial of difference, defense against difference, minimization of difference, acceptance of difference, adaptation to difference, and integration of difference. The 50-item psychometric Intercultural Developmental Inventory (IDI) has also been used to assess sensitivity in organizational leadership doctoral students, (Schmieder-Ramirez, Fortson, & Madjidi, 2005).

Technological Environment Analysis in SPELIT

Technology in this environment refers to the ability to improve surroundings. It also refers to the tools that individuals use to do tasks efficiently. It is not enough to just possess the tools (i.e., computers). You must also ensure that the infrastructure can support and educate those who use these tools. For example, China has been more successful in utilizing technology than Mexico because resources in China have been used to a greater extent to educate the populace regarding technology. Depending on the organization, you can do an analysis on how many individuals in an organization are skilled in the use of technology.

Practical Applications of the SPELIT Model

The SPELIT model can be used in any learning situation where it is important to know the environment first. Those who might use the model include student teachers, architect apprentices, law students, human resources consultants, or anyone in business that needs to assess the environment.

For example, in Clayton Christensen's analysis of the Butterfield Fabric Company, (1997), he notes that Butterfield had never formalized a strategy to meet the demands of change and were being bested by more focused competitors. The company used the *driving forces technique* outlined earlier in this chapter and divided these forces into competitive, technological, demographic, and economic forces that constitute threats or create opportunities. If the company had used the SPELIT model in combination with the driving forces, then the implications for strategy would have become obvious to the entire employee workforce.

In the non-profit sector, public school administrators as well as student teachers might utilize this model. A group of student teachers working in one school or the principal of the school might use SPELIT to work together on analyzing the aspects of the model impacting their school externally and internally. They can then analyze the driving forces that can either create an opportunity or threat to moving forward in their goals.

***

Summary

In this chapter we have reviewed the components of the SPELIT model and noted the theoretical basis which is a foundation for this model. Each component of the model was studied and the significant theorists were listed.

Finally practical applications were included for the reader. Teachers, organizational consultants, architects, and attorneys—anyone who needs to put together a learning plan or a strategy—would find this model extremely useful. It lays out each step and it involves the thinking of all those affected in any planned change.

***

References

Allison, G. (1971). *Essence of decision: Explaining the Cuban missile crisis.* New York: Little Brown Inc. (Republished in 1991).

Bennett, M.J. & Bennett, M. (2004). Developing intercultural sensitivity: An integrative approach to global and domestic diversity. In D. Landis, J. Bennett, & M. Bennett, (Eds.), Handbook of Intercultural Training. Pp. 147-166. Thousand Oaks, CA: Sage Publishing Co.

Bolman, L.G. & Deal. T. (1997), Reframing organizations: Artistry, choice and leadership, (2nd ed.)New York: Jossey Bass Inc.

Christensen, C. (1997). "Making strategy: Learning by doing," *Harvard Business Review* Nov./Dec. Issue.

Hammer, M.R. (1999). A measure of intercultural sensitivity: The Intercultural Development Inventory. In S.M. Fowler & M.G. Mumford (Eds.), Intercultural Sourcebook: Cross-cultural training methods (Vol. 2, pp. 61-72). Yarmouth, ME: Intercultural Press.

Hirschhorn, L. (1993). *The Psychodynamics of organizations..* Cambridge, MA: MIT Press.

Hofstede, G. (1980). *Culture's consequences: International differences in work-related Values.* Beverley Hills, CA: Sage.

Lewin, K. (1997). *Resolving social conflicts and field theory in social science.* Washington, D.C.: American Psychological Association.

Lewin, K. "Frontiers in group dynamics." *Human Relations,* 1947, 1,5-41.

Schein, E.H. (1985). *Organizational culture and leadership.* (2nd ed.)New York: Jossey Bass.

Senge, P. (1990). *The fifth discipline: The art and practice of the learning organization.*
New York: Doubleday.

Schmieder-Ramirez, J., Fortson, J. & Madjidi, (2004). Assessment of intercultural sensitivity of organizational leadership doctoral students utilizing the intercultural development inventory, (IDI). Educators and Scholars, 26(1).

Schon, D. (1983) *The reflective practitioner: How professionals think in action.* New York:
Basic Books.

Wenger, E. (1998). *Communities of practice: Learning, meaning and identity.*
SLondon: Cambridge University Press.

Chapter 2
Integrating Adult Learning and the SPELIT Analysis Methodology

Jacqueline B. Pritchett
Doctoral Student
Pepperdine University

In a democracy the people participate in making decisions that affect the entire social order. It is imperative, therefore, that every factory worker, every salesman, every politician, every housewife, know enough about government, economics, international affairs, and other aspects of the social order to be able to take part in them intelligently.
                                                                Malcolm S. Knowles

***

Introduction

At the core of humanity, there lies a profound need to acquire a thorough understanding of the world we live in. We explore the world through vast mental models, unique life experiences, and cultural frameworks. This exploring leads us from childhood to adulthood, and to further question our relevance in such a beautifully cosmic domain. As adults, we grow to find these answers within the family structure, religious and organizational affiliations, societal causes, and personal visions. The infinite need and relentless passion of humanity to seek answers to life's critical inquiries gradually becomes more complex and systematic as constant environmental changes affect our every move. Moreover, if we begin to comprehend and to embrace such a humane truth within ourselves then we must not ignore the will to seek and adapt relevant new ways of thinking, learning, and problem-solving in our ever-changing surroundings.

Malcolm S. Knowles, the father of adult learning and human resource development. He understood quite clearly the vital nature in which adults develop the capacity to think critically. Knowles and colleagues (1973, 1998) provided the world with a definitive model of andragogical adult learning theory, which includes core principles and conceptualities that frame how adults think and learn. According to Knowles, Holton, and Swanson (1998) these core principles of adult learning theory are as follows:

1. Learner's Need to Know
2. Self-Concept of the Learner
3. Prior Experience of the Learner
4. Readiness to Learn
5. Orientation to Learning, and
6. Motivation to Learn (p. 4)

In addition, there also exist internal and external core concepts associated with the adult learner that continuously influence their core principles, which include individual and situational differences as well as personal goals and purposes for learning (Knowles, et al, 1998).

In the spirit and tradition of andragogy and its aim at developing a better understanding of the adult learner, the SPELIT analysis methodology offers a new worthy systematic tool for today's adult learners and adult educators to take an opportunity to further evaluate yourself, others, and the external environment in order to transform your life, your organization, and society.

***

An Overview of the Chapter

The purpose of this chapter is to present a basic understanding of andragogy and to illustrate the importance of utilizing the SPELIT analysis methodology within an adult learning framework. Also, it is to demonstrate how adult learning theory and the SPELIT methodology complement one another in purpose and practice to offer the individual a new working paradigm to achieve personal, professional, and community growth. The chapter will introduce a historical glance of adult learning in the United States and an explanation of the core principles and concepts of adult learning theory. The chapter will highlight the unique characteristics of the adult learner and why today's adult learner needs the SPELIT analysis methodology to succeed in all aspects of life. The chapter will conclude with relevant examples of how every adult learner, educator, or business leader can put the SPELIT analysis methodology into practice to beget successful planned change.

***

Understanding Andragogy and the World of Adult Learning
A Brief Historical Perspective

Knowles (1969) declared that since the colonial period (1600-1779), settlers to the New World were driven by three forces that produced a powerful social consciousness of the value of education. These three primary forces are noted as: (a) the character of the immigrants coming into the New World focusing on its mass of opportunity, (b) the prominent protestant character of early American colonization, and (c) puritan ideology of engaging in constant steadfast behavior in the eyes of God (Knowles, 1969). Knowles also points out that as political agendas and social movements began to focus more on individual freedoms, citizenship and self-sustaining governments would require an educated society. Intellectual development could no longer be for the elite only class as in the mother country of Britain (Knowles, 1969).

The evolution of educating adults since the early 17th and 18th centuries began to take on many forms and involve a conglomeration of settings and outlets. Vocational education and apprenticeship system allowed adults to learn a trade to support themselves and their family. This kind of vocational learning was mainly designed for the poor in notes that what we know today as the university was the first permanent institutional form of education, Harvard College was founded by the Puritans of Massachusetts in 1652. Not all universities focused on adult learning from the onset; some like Harvard College were settings to train individuals such as ministers at the secondary school level (Knowles, 1969). Other institutions such as churches, libraries, and museums can be well-acknowledged in the wide-spread adult education movement in the United States.

During the 20th century, we witnessed a growth in defining what remarkable differences exist between youth learners and adult learners (Kidd, 1973; Kaufman, 1990; Knowles, 1950, 1998). This research crafted andragogy, the theory of adult learning. This gave learning theory new and powerfully dynamic theoretical frameworks beyond pedagogy, the theory of youth learning. This greatly mobilized the field of adult education. Andragogical theorists found that the adult learner was very unique and had much unrealized potential in the learning community.

Essentially, adult learners utilize their own set of internal and external motivators, social and philosophical ideologies, and methods of learning, including connecting to the world through expressed cognitive abilities such as critical thinking skills (Brookfield, 1986, 1987; Elias & Merriam, 1980; Knowles, 1950, 1998; Lowell, 1980).

In this next section we will meet the adult learner and gain more knowledge of their core principles and concepts towards learning.

***

The Adult Learner: Core Principles and Concepts

Adult learners possess a special set of cognitive abilities, experiences, values, and goals, which allows their full potential to thrive. However, drawing on the vast studies of adults and learning, we can firmly contend that there also exists a set of shared principles and values that bond together adult learners. Therefore, I will use the phrase *the adult learner* in order to indicate the holistic nature present in andragogy theory. Knowles et al. (1998) identifies the following six characteristics that richly describe adult learners:

1. Adult learners are self-directed and autonomous. They work well when given the freedom to direct their own work, set their own relevant goals, and become active participants in the learning process. It is essential for teachers of adults to continuously engage them in discussion-based instruction so that each may share their unique ideas, thoughts, and feelings about the subject matter. Teachers should become facilitators in an adult learning environment, allowing the adults to share actively in assigned leadership roles.
2. Adult learners possess an array of knowledge through their personal and professional life experiences. It is essential for adult learners to be able to intimately create continuity between class and real life situations. Teachers should bring to the forefront of each class experience significant links between methodologies, theories, and concepts and relevant real world examples to accomplish this connectivity for their adult learners.
3. Adult learners are goal-oriented in nature. Adults tend to understand what they want, need, and how to work toward their goals when entering the classroom. Teachers then should assist adults in achieving these goals by offering guidance through mentoring, coursework materials, and assignments that will further help frame their goals.
4 & 5. Adult learners are practical and relevancy-oriented. Teachers should create a course outline that makes sense to the

adult learner. With this, class responsibilities, expectations, and assignment deadlines should be clearly stated as well as open for inquiry if the adult learner presents cause for concern.
6. Adult learners should be granted respect by their instructors. Teachers should understand and recognize the uniqueness of each adult learner's worth as leaders in their families, work, and communities. Teachers should also be open to the complex viewpoints of each adult and respect them inside the classroom environment.

Moreover, Knowles et al. (1998) describes the six essential core principles and concepts that energize each adult in the learning environment as follows: (a) the learner's need to know, (b) self-directed learning, (c) prior experiences of the learner, (d) readiness to learn, (e) orientation to learning, and (f) motivation to learn (p. 4).

Knowles et al. (1998) suggests that there are three areas comprised within the "need to know" (p. 133) principle that include: "the need to know *how* learning will be conducted, *what* learning will occur, and *why* learning is important" (p. 133). An adult learner's *need to understand* the learning environment in which they will engage is apart of the shared control the learner requires to be more effective (Knowles et al. 1998).

To comprehend the core principle of adult learner as self-directing, Knowles et al. (1998) notes that there are two main concepts present within the literature: "First, self-directed learning is seen as self-teaching, whereby learners are capable of taking control of the mechanics and techniques of teaching themselves in a particular subject" (Knowles, et al, 1998). An illustration of self-teaching would be a student completing a home correspondence course by mail or a distance learning course online (Knowles, et al, 1996). Also, self-directed learning is believed to be a reflection of personal autonomy. Students control their own goals, purposes, and take personal ownership for their learning experience (Knowles, et al, 1996). Knowles et al contends that, "this leads to an internal change of consciousness in which the learner sees knowledge as contextual and freely questions what is learned" (p. 135).

The principle of prior experience of the learner is very relevant towards framing how effective andragogical-type learning will be for adults. Knowles et al (1998) notes four means by which an adult's prior experiences influence their learning. These include:

1. Create a wider range of individual differences.
2. Provide a rich resource for learning.
3. Create biases that can inhibit or shape new learning.
4. Provide grounding for adults' self-identity. (p. 139)

It is essential to identify any prior experiences that may have a negative impact on the adult learner and work towards improving perceptions and understanding of subject matter in order to create a more dynamic andragogical learning experience.

Knowles et al (1998) explains that "adults generally become ready to learn when their life situation creates a need to know" (p. 144). Therefore, to be more effective, it is of the utmost importance that adult educators become aware of and comprehend the varying life situations as well as circumstances and opportunities that suggest an adult's readiness to learn (Knowles, et al, 1998). Knowles, et al (1998) recommends *Pratt's Model of High and Low Direction and Support*, which will assist in recognizing the different levels of internal and/or external direction and support an adult may need in order to be ready for learning.

Furthermore, connected to readiness for learning means having a problem solving orientation toward learning rather than subject-centered learning (Knowles et al, 1998). Essentially, adults learn best when new learning is presented in a real-world context (Knowles, et al, 1998). With this in mind, Kolb (1984) defines learning as "the process whereby knowledge is created through transformation of experience" (as quoted in Knowles, et al, 1998, p. 146). Kolb's experiential learning model suggests four steps present in the experiential learning cycle (Knowles, et al). These are:

1. *Concrete experience*: full involvement in new here and now experiences.
2. *Observations and reflection*: reflection on and observation of the learner's experiences from many perspectives.
3. *Formation of abstract concepts and generalization*: creation of concepts that integrate the learners' observations into logically sound theories.
4. *Testing implications of new concepts in new situations*: using these theories to make decisions and solve problems. (p. 147)

Adult educators of all kinds in business and academia have embraced Kolb's experiential learning platform to enhance learning. Knowles, et al (1998) acknowledges that "the andragogical model of adult learning makes some fundamentally different assumptions about what motivates adults to learn" (p. 149). Consequently, most adults are motivated to learn if it helps them solve problems in the workplace or in their family life (Knowles, et al, 1998). Adult motivations for learning can also be very introspective and contribute to enhancing quality of life, self-esteem, personal satisfaction in learning, and cognitive stimulation (Knowles, et al, 1998). Moreover, adults can also be very extroversive such as engaging in professional networking, helping others, meeting new friends, and improving the social ills of mankind (Knowles, et al, 1998).

Each core principle presented in andragogy is consistent with core dynamics of the SPELIT methodology. In the following section, we will explore the important ways the SPELIT model can enhance the lives and learning of every adult learner.

***

Utilizing SPELIT in Adult Learning

In today's world, adult learners are bombarded with many challenges and extraordinary opportunities in the classroom, workplace, and home. There are a multitude of attributes of the external environment to ponder when arriving at a decision and/or solving a problem. To create positive odds for success takes a new way of thinking, a mental model paradigm shift in the way problems are handled and solved in business, in the classroom, and in the community. Senge (1990) explains that "mental models are deeply ingrained assumptions, generalizations, or even pictures or images that influence how we understand the world and how we take action; very often, we are not consciously aware of our mental models or the effects they have on our behavior" (p. 8). A *shift* is "to make change in or to change direction" (Webster's Ninth New Collegiate Dictionary, p. 1086). For adult learners, the SPELIT analysis methodology is a useful and systematic method to assist in developing such a shift in thinking and consequently a new way of seeing the world and themselves within it. The SPELIT analysis model will guide the thinking towards identifying and observing all the possible positives and negatives in any given situation.

The following scenario reflects how the SPELIT Interdisciplinary Analysis Methodology can guide adult learners, business leaders, and educators in getting a clear picture of where they are presently and how to systematically create solutions towards planned change for the future.

Samantha Stewart is a seasoned human resource (HR) recruiter at a non-profit organization for young women's leadership development. Samantha is a single mother of two wonderfully energetic children, Kate, 5 years old, and Sam, 10 years old. Recently, Samantha has heard that there will be changes in upper-management soon and many employees will be newly assigned and/or laid off throughout the entire organization. Samantha has a great professional record. She has scored high on all her 360 reviews throughout her 7-year tenure at the organization. Although a superb and dedicated worker, Samantha had concerns about how the change in management would affect her. Therefore, Samantha scheduled a conference with her manager, Ken, who has always supported Samantha and who has been with the organization for 12 years and completely understands what changes to expect from the new senior managers.

Samantha and Ken began their conference by outlining initial concerns she may have about her recruiting position. Ken reassures Samantha that the new senior managers know of her excellent record and invaluable contribution to the department as well as the entire organization. Samantha was relieved with the positive feedback; however, she wanted to expel one continuous rumor with Ken about the expectations of the new senior managers.

Samantha: "Ken, is it true that the new managers will require all senior HR recruiters to go back to school for further training?"

Ken: "Yes, actually they have been expressing the need for our senior human resource managers to attain an advanced master's degree in business, adult education, adult training, and/or human resources management."

Samantha: "Wow! Ken, I haven't been to school in 10 years and I have two kids in school; not to mention a heavy load of responsibility at work."

Ken: "I understand Samantha; you do have other options. For instance, we could offer you another position in another department that doesn't require a master's degree. However, you may lose some of your seniority as well as compromise all the great work you have been doing in recruitment for the organization."

Samantha: "I know, Ken. I am a little torn."

Ken: "If you want some advice from me, I believe you should think critically about all the possible benefits of this opportunity as well as any foreseen challenges you may face in order to come to a solution you will be satisfied with to move forward."

Samantha: "You are right. I need to clear my head and think. Thanks Ken!"

Ken: "You're welcome Samantha. Please let me know what you come up with and what direction you will take."

Samantha: "I surely will."

It is evident that Samantha has many different aspects of her personal and professional environments to think about in order to come to a suitable solution about whether to keep her current position as Senior HR recruiter. If Samantha utilized the SPELIT Interdisciplinary

Analysis Methodology to help guide her decision-making process, it could be described by Table 2-1. The SPELIT analysis methodology can clarify the present environment by bringing forth negative and positive effects, strengths and weakness, or pros and cons that will assist Samantha in making an informed decision about her career.

***

Summary

In this chapter, andragogy, the theory of adult learning, was discussed in order to understand the complex character of adults as life-long learners. We also explored the six core principles of adult learning involved in shaping the learner's goals and purposes, which include: (a) a learner's need to know, (b) self-concept of the learner, (c) prior experience of the learner, (d) readiness to learn, (e) orientation to learning, and (f) motivation to learn.

As adult learners, we must equip ourselves with methods that will assist our decision-making process throughout our personal lives, professions, and academic careers. As educational leaders, we must understand with totality our academic environment in order to create a more comprehensive learning experience within the classroom as well as foster worthy relationships with colleagues and the community. As business leaders within dynamic learning organizations, we must also think critically about inevitable influences that will determine a successful presence in today's domestic and global marketplaces. With such forward thinking, we can accomplish our vision, satisfy our consumers, and accomplish responsible long-term business and societal relationships.

The SPELIT analysis methodology was introduced in this chapter to illustrate a new and effective means of systematically processing the present environment to create clearly-defined solutions during times of anticipated planned change.

***

References

Brookfield, S. D. (1986). *Developing critical thinkers.* San Francisco: Jossey-Bass.

Brookfield, S. D. (1987). *Understanding and facilitating adult learning.* San Francisco: Jossey-Bass.

Elias, J. L., & Merriam, S. (1980). *Philosophical foundation in adult education.* Huntington, NY: Krieger Publishing Company.

Kaufman, A. S. (1990). *Assessing adolescent and adult intelligence.* Boston: Allyn and Bacon.

Kidd, J. R. (1973). *How adults learn.* New York: Association Press.

Knowles, S. M., Holton, F. E., & Swanson, A. R. (1998). *The adult learner: The definitive classic in adult education and human resource development.* (5th ed.). Houston, TX: Gulf Publishing Company.

Knowles, S. M., & Knowles, H. (1973). *Introduction to group dynamics.* Chicago: Follett.

Knowles, S. M. (1969). *The adult education movement in the United States.* New York: Holt, Rinehart, and Winston, Inc.

Knowles, S. M. (1950). *Informal adult education.* New York: Association Press.

Lowell, B. R. (1980). *Adult learning.* New York: Halsted Press.

Senge, M. P. (1990). *The fifth discipline. The art and practice of the learning organization.* New York: Doubleday Currency.

Schmieder-Ramirez, J., & Mallette, L. (2006). *An introduction to the SPELIT© interdisciplinary analysis methodology.* Pepperdine University.

Recommendations for Further Reading

Bash, L. (2003). *Adult learners in the academy.* Bolton: MA. Anker Publishing Company, Inc.

Galbraith, W. M. (ed.). (2004). *Adult learning methods: A guide for effective instruction* (3rd ed.). Malabar: FL. Krieger Publishing Company.

Knowles, S. M. (1975). *Self-directed learning: A guide for learners and teachers.*
New York: Association Press.

Merriam, S., & Caffarella, R. S. (1991). Learning in adulthood. San Francisco: Jossey-Bass.

Table 2-1
Utilizing the SPELIT Analysis Methodology in Samantha's Decision-Making Process

Drivers	Negative Effects	Positive Effects
Social	(-) Learning to become a graduate student and dealing with new college peers and professors' expectations. (-) Less quality time with the children. (-) Risking the loss of key relationships in HR department. (-) Risking the loss of seniority status in organization and HR department.	(+) Opportunity to learn more in the field of HR. (+) Opportunity to keep seniority status. (+) Building new relationships with new upper-management in current position. (+) Opportunity to network at the graduate level with other like-minded HR professionals. (+) Less responsibility in new assigned position, which may mean more free time with the children and time for other social endeavors.
Political	(-) Resistance from new upper-management regarding reassignment. (-) Resistance and backlash from HR staff and colleagues. (-) Starting from the beginning politically in another department or organization.	(+) Maintaining key relationships throughout the HR department and organization.
Economic	(-) Cost for paying for graduate classes and support materials. (-) Additional child care costs. (-) Possible pay reduction in new position.	(+) Organization reimburses for half of the cost of attendance. (+) Salary will remain the same in current position.
Legal	(-) New contractual agreement with child care agencies. (-) Filing more complicated tax returns with student status. (-) Confronting new HR legal policies and changing the current legality structure in the entire HR department.	(+) Tax benefits from being a student. (+) A more sophisticated legal structure for the HR department.
Intercultural	(-) Resistance in developing new diversity program implemented by new upper-management. (-) Time and effort implementing new diversity program throughout entire organization.	(+) Opportunity to create a new culturally aware work environment. (+) Opportunity to learn new information about cultures and organizational diversity.
Technological	(-) Upgrades to personal computer equipment to handle coursework requirements. (-) Possible costly upgrades to departmental equipment.	(+) Opportunity to create more efficient methods of working.

Part II
The SPELIT Environments

Part I of this book introduced the theorists that provide the fundamental building blocks for the SPELIT POWER MATRIX and an introduction to andragogy. Part II is based on the premise that *an organization can be evaluated by observing its environment.*

In chapter 3, Dr. Mallette expands upon the SPELIT analysis method described in chapter 1 to evaluate the environment of an organization, individuals, family, situations, a physical community, or a symbolic/virtual community such as a professional society. The individual environments are discussed in each of the succeeding chapters by a host of experts in their fields.

In chapter 4, Dr. Maier introduces us into the social environment.

In chapter 5, Dr. Schmieder-Ramirez presents the political environment.

In chapter 6, Dr. Lacourse and E. Martin talk about revenue and expenditures.

In chapter 7, Judge Tobin waxes poetic on the legal environment.

In chapter 8, G. Mazur and M. Moodian expose us to the intercultural environment.

In chapter 9, Dr. Shihadi discusses technology assessment.

In chapter 10, Dr. Mallette discusses other environments that might apply to specific situations or organizations.

Part III of this book will provide examples of the use of the SPELIT POWER MATRIX.

Chapter 3
The SPELIT Model

Dr. Leo A. Mallette, Program Manager

***

Introduction

An early political observer wrote that you could form an accurate opinion of a leader based on observing the people that support that leader (Machiavelli, 1515/1947). A variation of this could be: *An organization can be evaluated by observing its environment.* This book presents an analysis method to evaluate the environment of an organization, individuals, family, situations, a physical community, or a symbolic/virtual community such as a professional society. This technique is intended for practitioners doing a market analysis or diagnosis prior to implementing transitions or interventions and can be used by undergraduate students and seasoned practitioners. It can be used as a method of benchmarking your organization or another entity. This chapter will delineate a new environmental analysis technique. SPELIT is used to systematically analyze the social, political, economic, legal, intercultural, and technological environments of the entity to be analyzed (Figure 3-1).

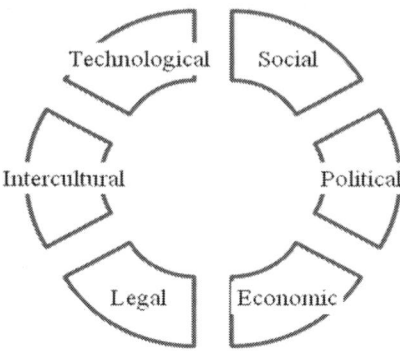

Figure 3-1. Environments Analyzed by the SPELIT POWER MATRIX

The social environment involves people-to-people interactions. The political environment revolves around power. The economic environment looks at the production and consumption of resources. The legal environment involves contracts and the law. The intercultural environment considers factors of collaboration in a global setting. The technology environment interprets the advancements of the scientific revolution.

This chapter will build on the work of major change and adult learning theorists. The individual elements of this analysis method are described briefly below and in detail in chapters 4 through 9.

All the theories mentioned in the Introduction and the Theory Chapter include (or infer) a step for analysis or diagnosis of the current environment that *defines the way things are now*. The SPELIT analysis methodology is used to systematically analyze the environment of an organization such as a family, a company such as General Motors, individuals such as your boss, a decision such as marriage or graduate school, a physical community such as a home owner's association, or a symbolic community such as a professional society, for example, the American Educational Research Association (AERA).

An organization can be evaluated by observing its environment.

Environment

There are different ways to describe perspectives about the environment. Bolman & Deal (2003, p. 19) listed terms such as schemata or schema, representations, cognitive maps, paradigms, social categorization, implicit theories, mental models, root metaphors, and frames. Christiansen (1997) used the terms mapping and factors. We simply use the term *environments* to describe the elements of the SPELIT analysis model.

Many theorists systematically evaluate the environment of an organization, if for no other reason than to have a baseline to measure if change occurred after an intervention. The next section describes an analysis methodology to implement an environmental evaluation.

***

SPELIT Environmental Assessment

SPELIT is an acronym for social, political, economic, legal, intercultural, and technological. The first step in many change or transition theories is to quantify the existing environment. This can be analyzed using the six-environment SPELIT analysis tool. All six perspectives or environments may not be needed, and some of the topics can be eliminated or weighted differently. Figure 3-2 shows the six environments equally weighted.

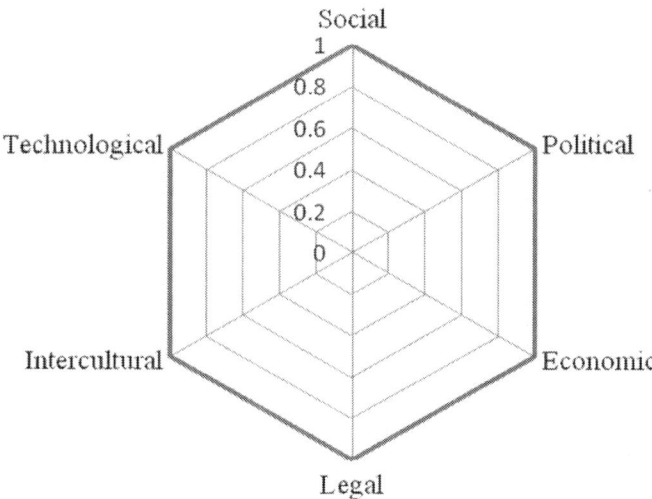

Figure 3-2. Some SPELIT Environments may be Assigned More Importance Than Others, or the Same as in this Illustration.

The economics environment might be eliminated if resources are not an issue. Similarly, the intercultural environment might be eliminated if all individuals are monocultural. Similarly, other specialized environments can be added as discussed in chapter 10. The six major environments of the SPELIT model are introduced here and expanded upon in the following chapters.

Sociology is the study of how people behave in various group interactions, such as work, home, family, church, sports teams, driving, and so on (Macionis, 2004). The SPELIT social environment addresses the social character of an organization and is discussed in Chapter 4: The Social Environment.

Politics is the process of making decisions within groups and is closely tied to the concepts of power and influence. These groups can be governments, but a political environment is associated with any group of people. The SPELIT political environment can address organizational structure and sources of power (legitimate, referent, expert, and coercive). This is discussed in chapter 5: the *Political Environment*.

Economics is concerned with production and consumption of resources. The SPELIT economics environment addresses resources of an organization such as facilities, trucks, people, goodwill, or money. This is discussed in chapter 6: the *Economics Environment*.

The legal environment includes official laws or accepted rules. The legal system can be based on civil law, common law, customary law, and religious law. The SPELIT legal environment addressed the laws, customs, and ethics of the organization. This is discussed in chapter 7: the *Legal Environment*.

Being interculturally sensitive "is to be aware of the points of view of others and to recognize differences in cultures" (J. Schmieder-Ramirez, Fortson, & Madjidi, 2004, p. 7). The SPELIT intercultural environment addresses culture and differences between cultures that would be a driver for an organization. This is discussed in chapter 8: the *Intercultural Environment*.

Technology is the use of tools that humans have developed to become more efficient, and technology is driving how everyone does business. Tools can be as simple as a pin, or as complex as the space shuttle. This is discussed in chapter 9: the *Technological Environment*.

Other Environments

There are other aspects of organizations and people that could be considered environments or factors that cannot be nicely categorized. For example, should the ethics of a person be categorized into the social, legal, or intercultural environment? This topic is further discussed in chapter 10: *Environmental Epilogue*.

***

Summary

The SPELIT analysis methodology was introduced in this chapter. This technique is intended for practitioners doing a market analysis or diagnosis prior to implementing transitions or interventions. It can be used by undergraduate students and seasoned practitioners. This methodology aligns with established and more current theories. It delineates a new environmental analysis technique that is used to systematically analyze the social, political, economic, legal, intercultural, and technological environments.

The next chapter will discuss the social environment of SPELIT.

***

References

Bolman, L., & Deal, T. (2003). *Reframing organizations, Artistry, choice, and leadership.* San Francisco CA: Jossey-Bass.

Bridges, W. (2003). *Managing transitions* (2nd ed.). Cambridge, MA: Da Capo Press.

Bygrave, W., & Zacharakis, A. (2004). *The portable MBA in entrepreneurship* (3rd ed.). Hoboken, NJ: John Wiley & Sons.

Christiansen, C. M. (1997). Making strategy: Learning by doing. *Harvard Business Review*, 3-12.

Cummings, T., & Worley, C. (2005). *Organization development & change* (8th ed.). Mason, OH: South-Western.

Geisen, C., Evans, L., Mallette, L. A., & Suwandee, A. (2005). *Organizational analysis tools to identify possible cause and corrective action for lack of collaboration between principals in a private school.* Paper presented at the Hawaii International Conference on Education, Honolulu HI.

Holcomb, E. (2001). *Asking the right questions: Techniques for collaboration and school change.* Thousand Oaks CA: Corwin Press.

Kaufman, J. (2000). *Mega planning: Practical tools for organizational success.* Thousand Oaks CA: Sage.

Lewin, K. (1951). *Field theory in social science.* New York: Harper & Row.

Machiavelli, N. (1515/1947). *The prince* (T. G. Bergin, Trans.). New York NY: Appleton-Century-Crofts.

Macionis, J. J. (2004). *Sociology* (10th ed.). New York NY: Prentice Hall.

McCall, C. H. (2002). *Understanding statistical methods, A manual for students and data analysts.* San Jose, CA: Writers Club Press.

Schmieder-Ramirez, J., Fortson, J. L., & Madjidi, F. (2004). Assessment of intercultural sensitivity of organizational leadership doctoral students utilizing the intercultural development inventory (IDI). *Scholar and Educator, the Journal of the Society of Educators and Scholars, 26*(1).

Wikipedia. (2006). *Technology.* Retrieved January 12, 2006 from http://en.wikipedia.org/wiki/Technology

Chapter 4
On the Social Aspects of Organization: "The Human Side of Enterprise" Revisited

Mark Maier, Ph.D.
Founding Chair, Leadership & Organization Studies Program
Chapman University

Administration (n.): From the Latin, ad (to promote) and ministrare (service, as in "to minister"). Literally, "to promote service."
—From Webster.

The conventional definition of management is getting work done through people, but real management is developing people through work.
—Agha Hasan Abedi

Humanitarianism consists of this principle: That no man is sacrificed to an end.
—Albert Schweitzer

The work exists for the person as much as the person exists for the work.
—Robert K. Greenleaf

***

Introduction

In this chapter, we focus on the sociological and social psychological underpinnings of organization: The fundamentals of how people interact with one another and how the structures they create impact how they interact with one another. We shall examine some of the fundamental assumptions of human behavior in organizations—most notably motivation—and explore how conventional forms of organizing (hierarchy, bureaucracy) and managing (planning, organizing, directing, controlling) undermine leadership and organizational effectiveness. We shall conclude with contrasting case studies of Southwest Airlines and NASA to illustrate the implications of the social perspective in the SPELIT POWER MATRIX for leadership and organizational effectiveness.

***

The Fundamental Question "Y": Reflections on the Purpose and Features of Organization

Core assumptions of the social perspective, taking into account both human resource and structural frames (Bolman & Deal, 1997: 40; 102-103), include:

1. a. Organizations exist to serve human needs.
   b. Organizations exist to achieve established goals and objectives.
2. People and organizations need each other.
3. Structures must be designed to fit an organization's circumstances.
4. Organizations can increase efficiency and enhance performance through focus on rationality, task specialization, and the division of labor (Weber, 1946; Bolman & Deal 1997: 40).

Appropriate forms of coordination and control are necessary to ensure that individuals and units work together in the service of organizational goals. Since the advent of large-scale organizations in the 19th century, practitioners have tended to overemphasize the task side of the enterprise, with a concomitant—and enduring—neglect of the human side. As Douglas McGregor, one of the chief 20th Century critics of this tendency explained more than 50 years ago:

> We must now learn how to utilize the social sciences to make our human organizations truly effective. The philosophy of management by direction and control is inadequate to motivate....Direction and control are essentially useless in motivating people whose important needs are social and egoistic. (McGregor, 1957, cited in Shafritz & Ott, 2001: 179/182)

Readers may be surprised to recognize the salience of McGregor's insights *50 years later.* That his words still ring true today speaks to the power of the industrial model of management—a 19th Century worldview—to continue to shape managerial action and organizational behavior in the 21st Century. In articulating a classic distinction between this conventional approach (what he called "Theory X"), and a more enlightened alternative ("Theory Y"), McGregor discussed the role that managers should play in "creating opportunities, releasing potential, removing obstacles, encouraging growth, providing guidance" (in Shaftritz & Ott, 2001: p. 183). Abandoning "management by control," in McGregor's view, rested on an assumption that people were *not* by nature passive or resistant to organizational needs, but have "become so *as a result of* experience in organizations." (Shafritz & Ott, 2001: p. 183, emphasis added) The conventional approach, he observed, was (and is!) based on "mistaken notions of what is cause and what is effect." (p. 180)

McGregor, whose enduring contribution was to stress "the human side of enterprise," was certainly not the first to lay claim to that territory. Mary Parker Follett, for example, in the 1920s had already issued stinging critiques of Henri Fayol's (1916) and Frederick Winslow Taylor's (1911) perspectives on the primacy of managerial control, arguing that the wish to govern your own life constituted "the very essence of the human being." (in Shafritz & Ott, 2001: p. 155) And Fritz Roethlisberger's famous reports (1941) on the Hawthorne Experiments similarly demonstrated the criticality of the human element in organizations, that people were essentially meaning-seeking organisms: "Most of us want the satisfaction that comes from being accepted and recognized as people of worth by our friends and work associates...We all want tangible evidence of our social importance." (in Shafritz & Ott, 2001: p. 165-166)

Abraham Maslow's (1943) theory of human motivation was that "higher level needs" (e.g., for love, esteem, and self-actualization) became salient when people's "lower level needs" (physiological/survival, safety) were met. Building on Maslow's theory, McGregor stressed that these motivations "are all present in people," by which he meant "the potential for development, the capacity for assuming responsibility, the readiness to direct behavior toward organizational goals" (in Shafritz & Ott, p. 183). In other words, management "does not put them there" (p. 183). Fifty years after he penned these prescient observations, you might wonder why they have not been more widely taken to heart.

"It is the responsibility of management to make it possible for people to recognize and develop these human characteristics for themselves," McGregor concluded, and that the essential task of management was to "arrange organizational conditions and methods of operation so that people can achieve their own goals *best* by directing *their own* efforts toward organizational objectives." (p. 183.) In short, the conventional approach (Theory X) relies upon *external* control of behavior, while a more enlightened—human-centered—approach (Theory Y) relies on an *internal* focus (self-control, self-direction).

From a sociological perspective, you can examine the particular configuration of an organization's social architecture: The horizontal division of labor and specialization of tasks and the vertical arrangement of the chain of command and reporting lines. Delving deeper, you can examine not only *how* an organization is structured in a particular way and with what *consequences*, but *why* (i.e., whose interests are served by that configuration and whose are *not* served).

Once an organizational structure is in place and individual roles are specified (by position, location, and activity), coordination is achieved by both (1) vertical and (2) lateral means. As Bolman & Deal summarize, vertical mechanisms for coordinating the work of organizations include devices such as (a) formal authority (chain of command), (b) rules, policies and procedures, and (c) planning and control systems (e.g., performance plans, action plans). (Bolman & Deal, 1997: 42-43). Lateral devices include meetings, task forces, and the establishment of coordinating units, matrix structures, or computer networks.

From a structural vantage point, the following organizational dilemmas are commonly observed: (1) the more differentiated a structure is, the harder it is to integrate; (2) there can be excessive overlap of responsibilities or, conversely, gaps created if all necessary responsibilities are not clearly assigned. A colleague of mine in the Organizational Behavior Teaching Society, for example, once characterized organizations as "vast systems of organized irresponsibility." Other structural dilemmas identified by Bolman and Deal (1997) include: "underuse versus overload...lack of clarity versus lack of creativity...excessive autonomy versus excessive interdependence...too loose versus too tight...diffuse authority versus overcentralization...goal-less versus goal-bound...irresponsible versus unresponsive." (p. 60-61).

The key organizational processes, from a social perspective, that must be balanced are (1) autonomy and community (individuation and integration), (2) differentiation and homogenization (specialization and commonality), and (3) stability (continuity) and change (adaptability). (Oshry 1994, 1999).

Summing up the Social Aspects of Organization: Key Drivers

The key drivers that emerge from an understanding of this perspective include awareness, relationships, and an over-riding service orientation. The social aspects focus draws our attention to both the inner as well as outer work of leaders (Cashman, 1998; Wilber, 2000; Klein, 2006).

(1) Awareness. An acute awareness of self, of others, of your environment (situation and context) is stressed. *Emotional intelligence* (Goleman, 1998) is acknowledged and developed, resulting in a communication stance oriented toward mutual learning, as opposed to an orientation toward imposed will. This includes moving from reliance on technical rationality to "reflection-in-action" (Schoen, 1983). Emotional intelligence can be distinguished by two forms of competence: (1) Personal competence (the way in which we manage ourselves in various circumstances) and (2) Social competence (how we handle relationships).

Personal competencies, according to Goleman, include self-awareness, self-regulation, and motivation. *Self-awareness* refers here to "knowing one's inner states, preferences, resources, and inhibitions" (Goleman, 1998, p. 26) and consists of emotional awareness (recognizing your emotions and their effects), *accurate* self-assessment (knowing your strengths and limits), and self-confidence (sense of self-worth and capabilities). *Self-regulation* refers to how you manage your internal states, impulses, and resources. Self-regulation consists of self-control (e.g., keeping disruptive emotions in check), trustworthiness, conscientiousness, adaptability (flexibility in handling change), and innovation (e.g., being comfortable with new ideas and approaches). *Motivation* implies emotional tendencies that guide or facilitate reaching goals and is comprised of the following: achievement drive, commitment, initiative, and optimism (e.g., the ability to persist in pursuing goals despite obstacles and setbacks).

Social competencies include *empathy* (an awareness of others' feelings, needs, and concerns) and *social skills* (adeptness at "inducing desirable responses in others") according to Goleman (1998: p. 27). *Empathy* is comprised of such competencies as understanding others, developing others, service orientation, leveraging diversity, and political awareness. *Social skills* include influence, communication (listening openly), conflict management, leadership, being a change catalyst, building bonds, collaborating and cooperating, and developing team capabilities (group synergy). (Goleman, 1998: p. 27)

(2) Focus on Relationships. "Relationships are primary, everything else is derivative," my colleague, Marty Linsky, of Harvard once reminded me. From a social perspective, a prime driver in accounting for organizational dynamics and performance is the extent to which human needs for connection are being met. A stance of respect for others and inclusiveness prevails. *Appreciative Inquiry* (Hammond, 1998) is encouraged and practiced; others are empowered. A premium is placed on process and means versus goals and ends. (Enabling

human needs for achievement, replacing fear and reactive responses with passion and creative responses). As Blanchard and O-Connor highlighted in their best-selling *Managing by Values* (1997), the pathway to principle-centered organizations requires integrating (1) connection and (2) achievement.... In that order.

(3) Service. The third principal driver from a social perspective has to do with organizational purpose. Specifically, is there an orientation to serve others and commitment to their highest development? Are members committed to a purpose beyond themselves? Robert Greenleaf (1991) put this challenge into stark relief when he proposed that leading be seen as a way of serving, that for "the servant as leader,"

> ...it begins with a natural feeling that one wants to serve, to serve *first*. Then conscious choice brings one to aspire to lead. This is sharply different from the person who it *leader* first, perhaps because of the need to assuage an unusual power drive or to acquire material possessions. For this person it will be a later choice to serve—if the choice is made at all—after leadership has been established." (p. 7, emphasis original)

The difference between these two archetypes for Greenleaf manifested itself in the extent to which—consistent with the social aspects of the organization model being elucidated here—other people's highest priority needs are being served. According to Greenleaf (1991),

> The best test, and difficult to administer, is: Do those served grow as persons? Do they, *while being served*, become healthier, wiser, freer, more autonomous, more likely themselves to become servants? *And*, what is the effect on the least privileged in society; will they benefit, or at least, not be further deprived? (p.7, emphasis original)

Greenleaf's experience at AT&T and as founder in 1970 of the Center for Applied Ethics (now the Greenleaf Center for Servant Leadership), led him to some of the same conclusions that Douglas McGregor had reached about the transformative capability of putting people and their development first. If organizations were to re-channel "the ingenuity and perseverance of industrial management in the pursuit of economic ends" and apply those same talents to the human side of enterprise, McGregor opined, not only would this "enhance substantially of these materialistic achievements, but will bring us one step closer to 'the good society'." (in Shafritz & Ott, 2001: p. 184). Given the dominance of the workplace and work routines in modern life, it might surprise readers to learn that Greenleaf—like McGregor before him—was ultimately more concerned not with narrow organizational performance per see, but with its *implications* for the kind of society we create. After all, since most people in the western world spend the majority of their waking hours devoted to the work sector, the quality of that experience would—according to Greenleaf—have the potential to transform society itself. This was his de facto credo:

> If a good society is to be built, one that is more just and more caring and providing opportunity for people to grow...the most effective way is to raise the performance-as-servants of *institutions*, and sanction natural servants to serve and lead. (quoted in Frick & Spears,1996: p. 5, emphasis added)

This shift in thinking and focus has tremendous implications for how organizations operate. Table 4-1 summarizes the key dimensions of the social aspects of organization.

Organizational Consequences Seen Through the Lens of the Social Perspective

The conventional managerial paradigm (emphasizing results, direction, control, prerogative) and the exigencies of pyramidal politics and organizational hierarchy induces organizational participants alike to "follow in the footsteps" of their misguided predecessors. The educator's responsibility is to prepare them to lead and organize in fundamentally different ways, ways which emphasize service over self-interest (Block, 1993; Greenleaf, 1991) and networks of collaboration over pyramids of control (Wheatley, 1996 ; Helgesen, 1991).

It is imperative for educators to be able to identify, articulate, and promote alternatives to this paradigm and the "pyramidal politics" (Block, 1987) it promotes. According to Block, the conventional bureaucratic/hierarchical social architecture inexorably induces the following predictable effects on individual and interpersonal behavior:

(1) It relies fundamentally on a "patriarchal contract"—a "top-down, high-control orientation" (Block, 1987: 22) in which organizational participants perceive—and are rewarded for so-perceiving—that your survival and advancement depends upon pleasing your "dad" in the system (i.e., your boss).
(2) This, in turn, reinforces a "myopic self-interest" so that participants are encouraged to think of themselves and their careers ("moving up the ladder") first, foremost, and only.
(3) As a result, this encourages an essential dependency on the part of organizational "subordinates" on those situated above them in the hierarchy.

(4) This in turn gives rise to "manipulative tactics," completing "the bureaucratic cycle." This cycle, according to Block, unintentionally encourages people "to choose to maintain what they have, to be cautious and dependent." (p. 21)

Block's observations echo Robert K. Merton's (1957) analysis of the relationship between bureaucratic structure and personality, in which the conventional structure promotes "overconformity" (submissiveness) and rewards tendencies for "ascendancy" (advancement). Merton was wise to point out that for all of the purported advantages of bureaucratic structure (precision, reliability, efficiency), there are corresponding liabilities and limitations (e.g., lack of creativity, obedience, and means-ends displacement—where the rules become ends in themselves).

Bolman and Deal take note of this as well: The specialization of labor and the hierarchical division of authority encourages "a fundamental passivity" among those at lower levels, a tendency which intensifies "as one moves down the hierarchy" (Bolman & Deal, 1997: p. 108) and as participants mature. The frustrations associated with the lack of control over your environment, and the lack of respect and engagement accorded to participants at lower levels, can give rise to many outcomes, including (1) physical withdrawal (absenteeism, quitting); (2) psychological withdrawal (indifference, passivity, apathy); (3) restricting output, deception, sabotage; (4) advancement (climb the hierarchy to attempt to increase control), (5) forming groups to address power imbalance (e.g., unionizing). (See, for example, Argyris 1957; 1974).

Creating the Future We Desire:
Implications of the Social Perspective for Management and Leadership

It is axiomatic that organizations exist to serve a purpose, but which purpose? Whose purpose? Rather than taking the narrow economic model for granted (e.g., that corporations exist to maximize profit for shareholders) we assume here that organizations—*all* organizations (including for-profit corporations!)—exist to serve human needs. To the extent that corporations deliver on that service, they earn profit. As A. P. Giannini, the founder of the Bank of America, explained, "Serving the needs of others is the only legitimate business in the world today." And though profit is essential to corporate survival, it cannot be confused with the corporation's *reason for being*, its core purpose. Organizations that cannot resolve that confusion operate blindly and implode fantastically. For example, Enron, Worldcom, and TYCO are recent examples of the obsessive focus on the bottom line run amok.

Table 4-1
Contrasting Implications of the Social Aspects of Organization

Dimension	Subordinates Human Factor	Attends to Human Factor
Organizational Metaphor	Pyramid, Hierarchy (Bureaucracy)	Circle, Network (Web)
Era	Industrial Age; Machine Era (Mechanistic)	Information Age; Service Era (Organic)
Orientation to Organization	Segmented: Work	Holistic: Life/Work integration
Energy Focus & Stance	Preserve self; advance career. Fear; Safety; Anxiety Conflict tension (Reactive)	Create what matters most. Passion, Courage; Meaning Creative Tension (Creative)
Needs Addressed	Power, achievement, advancement (ranking)	Love, affiliation; Connection (linking)
Competencies Stressed	Technical Skills, Task capability; IQ	Social and Self-Awareness skills; Emotional Intelligence
Adaptive/Correction Strategies	Managing as directing: Critical; deficit-focus	Leading as serving: Appreciative Inquiry
Motivational Emphasis	External; Materialistic; Egoistic	Internal; Actualization (of Self & Others)
Guiding Principles/Values	Success (ends); Efficiency; Control; Use others	Service (means); Effectiveness; Empowerment; Grow/Develop others
Human Resource Practices	Enforce compliance	Inspire commitment
Interpersonal Communication	Impose point of view; Advocacy – Winning (Competitive)	Mutual learning; Dialogue - Exchanging (Collaborative)
Ultimate Objective	Performance; Individual Achievement; Organizational Profit	Performance + Fulfillment; Serve & Enhance Society

Arie de Geuss, the legendary head of worldwide planning for Royal Dutch/Shell, explained that this amounts to confusing a prerequisite for organizational survival with its reason for being. "Companies need profits in the same way as any living being needs oxygen. It is a necessity to stay alive, but it is not the purpose of life." And, as Peter Senge and his associates point out in their best-selling *Fifth Discipline Fieldbook* (1994) every profit-making corporation has the purpose of making money, therefore focusing on that purpose, at the expense of others, distracts from an organization's competitive advantage; what makes it unique. This point has also been more recently corroborated in Collins & Porras's excellent research into companies of enduring greatness, those that are "Built to Last" (1997). Or, as Ken Blanchard and Norman Vincent Peale (1988) put it in their famous essay, *The Power of Ethical Management* "managing only for profit is like playing tennis with your eye on the scoreboard and not on the ball. Sometimes when the numbers look right," they caution, "the decision is still wrong." (p. 106) In short, only if we are aware of what our true purpose is can we live (i.e., lead!) a principle-centered life. As Robert Greenleaf, the founding director of management development at AT&T and subsequent pioneer of the servant-leadership model, proclaimed that you must first accept "that means determine the ends." (Frick & Spears, 1996: 101).

> A search for the capabilities and possibilities in people is gradually supplanting the search for the liabilities. It is a more optimistic philosophy. An important weakness in the concept of the single chief at the top of a managerial hierarchy is that such a person is apt to be a manager and to assume, by virtue of having the position, that he or she has all the talents it requires. (Greenleaf, as cited in Frick & Spears, p. 101)

Attending to the human factor in organizations allows you us to draw essential distinctions between management as it is conventionally conceived and as it might be. Indeed, it allows us to draw clear distinctions between *managing* and *leading* (see Rost, 1991), as I have discussed elsewhere (Maier, 1998) and summarize in Table 4-2.

From the perspective of the social aspects of an organization, we can conceive of the managerial role much more broadly. Where managing is conventionally considered an instrumental activity, a way of *doing* (e.g., "How do I get others to do X, Y, or Z in order to advance outcome A, B, or C?"). In contrast, leadership can be conceptualized as an expression of *identity*—a way of *being*, one which may clearly fall within the purview of *any* organizational member (not just managers!).

Table 4-2
Exploring the Implications of the Social Aspects of Organization: Contrasting the Essence of Management and Leadership. Adapted from Maier (1998).

MANAGEMENT	LEADERSHIP
An authority relationship ...	An influence relationship ...
between "managers" and "subordinates" (fixed by position),	between "leaders" and "followers" (interchangeable, dynamic – open to anyone),
reflecting an *administrative* function	reflecting an *interpersonal process*
whose purpose is set by management.	which reflects *mutual* purposes.
An inherently *coercive* activity (implicit or explicit),	An inherently *voluntary* activity,
whose focus is *maintaining* the organization (producing goods or services; coordinating, smooth running)	Which *intends real change* (growing or building the organization)
so that "bottom line" objectives and goals are met (results-oriented).	so that the vision, mission, and values of the organization are clarified and advanced ("top line"; purpose-oriented).

As reflected in Table 4-1, If you understand that the principles of scientific management emerged from the machine age (and its technological embodiment, the industrial revolution) and from our best understanding of science and "how the world worked" at the time (Newtonian perspectives of cause and effect; reducing operations to the sum of their parts), then you can imagine the implications of our *current* understanding of science (quantum and chaos theory, complexity theory, systems theory) for organizational behavior. The science of chaos "teaches us that order can emerge out of a seemingly chaotic system if we understand the underlying principles that can produce that order." (Kim, 2002 p. 17; see also Wheatley & Kellner-Rogers, 1996; Lewin & Regine, 2000; Johnson, 1997). Two such implications lie (1) in the attention not only to your technical skills and IQ, but your "emotional intelligence" (Goleman, 1998), as we elaborated upon above and (2) the attention to underlying structures which produce surface-level organizational events, as represented in Table 4-3.

LEVERAGE	**INTERVENTION FOCUS**	**ACTION MODE**
Lowest	Events	Reactive
	Patterns of Behavior	Adaptive
Higher	Systemic Structures	Creative
	Mental Models	Reflective
Highest	Vision	Generative

Table 4-3
Action Mode Options as a Function of Perspective Level: Increasing Leverage for Action in the Social Aspects of Organization. Source: Daniel Kim (2002), reprinted with permission of the Greenleaf Center for Servant Leadership.

As Kim (2002) explains, when we respond simply to the events of our day, we are engaging in *reactive* actions. However, living only at the events level is limiting, Kim explains, because at this level all we do is react to what is happening. If we can discern *patterns*, we increase our leverage for creating the future we desire because we able to *adapt* to the patterns we identify. We can *anticipate* events before they occur and adjust our actions accordingly. But even here, as Kim points out, we are not focused on creating the future we desire but still responding to what is happening to us.

If we can shift our focus to the level of systemic structures, we begin to identify the *source* of the patterns and events we have been responding to at the surface level. If we want to change those patterns, we must take *creative* actions to modify those structures (or create new ones). As Kim points out, however, even if you *do* succeed in creating new structures, your effectiveness will depend on the extent to which your deep beliefs—your mental models

> are aligned with the changes in the system's structures. The Achilles heel of most change efforts (studies have shown that over two thirds fail to produce the desired results) is that they do not move beyond this level to engage the organization at the level of mental models. (Kim 2002: p. 10)

Therefore, if we are really committed to effecting enduring changes, the level of mental models *must* be engaged. To engage this level requires *reflective* actions, "actions that require us to surface, suspend, and test our deepest beliefs" of how we see our world. (p. 11) Finally, as Kim concludes, "unless we are deeply connected to a vision that we care about bringing into reality," (p. 11) we are unlikely to undertake that work. This is why *generative* actions—those which generate the results we desire—ultimately matter the most, for they hold the power to "reconnect us to our sense of purpose and to visions we care deeply about." (p. 11) Leading from these points of higher leverage is essential if we are truly concerned about creating the future we desire.

***

Applications of the Social Perspective: Contrasting Case Studies
Southwest Airlines vs. NASA

Neglecting the Social Aspects Perspective: A Negative Case Study in NASA

A close study of the space shuttle *Challenger* and *Columbia* disasters—though 17 years and 66 missions apart—reveals striking parallels. These similarities were so pronounced that the official Columbia Accident Investigation Board's (CAIB, 2003) final report devoted an entire section to dissecting the managerial actions which culminated in the death of the Columbia Crew. The title of that section was "Echoes of Challenger." The managerial critique offered by the CAIB (pronounced "cabe") represents, in essence, a ringing condemnation of a social system operating not abnormally, but absolutely normally, at least within the conventional paradigm of management and organization which still (pre)dominates. This resulted in high-profile SNAFU's (Situation Normal: All Fouled Up) which produced not one, but two space shuttle disasters. Here is a brief synopsis of how managers and an organization operating "normally" was, in fact, operating in ways which were deficient and dysfunctional, to the point of disaster.

Challenger failed in January 1986 because repeated attempts to alert key decision-makers of the inherent dangers of the solid rocket boosters' o-ring sealing capability fell on deaf ears. Why? Applying the root-cause analysis and insights highlighted by the Social Aspects of Organizations framework (Table 4-1) and Kim's (2002) analysis, we see that managers were more preoccupied with meeting an artificial timetable to accelerate the launch schedule from 9 flights in 1985 to 15 flights in 1986, and up to 24 by 1990, than with flight safety. Warnings that record-cold temperatures at lift-off would compromise the ability of the rockets' o-rings to seal properly were also submerged because such news was anathema to managers' mental models: (1) that o-rings could not be a "safety of flight" issue; and (2) that the space agency was already committed to bringing a secondary launch facility "on line" at Vandenberg AFB in California where cold temperatures in the range at issue on the Challenger launch (as low as 58 degrees) are commonplace. Hundreds of millions of dollars had been invested in that effort, and no one wanted to be responsible for bursting NASA's bubble, regardless of what the reality dictated. In a famous telephone conference meeting between NASA and the rocket contractor, NASA managers bristled at the suggestion of a low-temperature launch constraint: "My God, Thiokol! When do you expect me to launch? Next April?!" Unwilling to take the risk of alienating their major customer, Thiokol reversed their "no-launch" recommendation, even though their top experts were opposed. When asked why they did not even poll their engineers in a private caucus on the final decision, Thiokol managers asserted incredulously: "We only polled the management people because we had already established that we were not going to be unanimous." (Maier, 1992)

Similarly, 17 years later, *Columbia's* foam shedding problem presented an unwelcome challenge to NASA managers struggling once more to meet—you guessed it—an arbitrary deadline of completing the core module of the International Space Station by February 19, 2004. So obsessed were NASA managers with meeting that projected target date that all concerns with foam damage were interpreted within a mental model of a threat to the schedule, not as a threat to flight safety or human life. NASA's engineers' requested that the Department of Defense to train one of our vaunted spy satellites onto the underbelly of the shuttle to assess the damage of the "foam strike" that had hit the leading edge of the left-hand wing. The request was "turned off" by their superiors who were more concerned with an apparent breach of protocol and procedure because the request had not been "vetted" through proper channels. Had that request been allowed to proceed, they would have discovered a hole larger than a basketball on the underside of the wing and would have been able to pull out all the stops in an *Apollo-13* ("failure is not an option")-type rescue effort. However, the NASA manager in charge simply asserted that even if there were a severe problem "there is nothing we could do about it anyway," thus setting in motion a catastrophic incidence of a self-fulfilling prophecy.

In its analysis of the twin disasters, the Columbia Accident Investigation Board (CAIB) found numerous structural and bureaucratic parallels: "NASA's culture of bureaucratic accountability emphasized chain of command, procedure, following rules, and going by the book. The unintended negative effect: Allegiance to hierarchy and procedure replaced deference to NASA engineers' technical expertise." (2003, p. 200) In further observations on "History as Cause: Echoes of Challenger," CAIB found that NASA's structure and hierarchy "blocked effective communication. Signals were overlooked, people were silenced, and useful information and dissenting views of technical issues did not surface at higher levels." (p. 201).

In both cases, "what was communicated to parts of the organization was that o-ring erosion and foam debris were not problems." (p. 201). Had NASA been configured in ways more attuned to the social aspects of organization presented here, then both tragedies could have been averted. If you accept the common definition of insanity—"Doing the same thing over and over and expecting a different result"—Here are some suggestions CAIB made to prevent such insanity (CAIB, 2003, pp. 195-204):

- Leaders create culture. It is also the leaders' responsibility to change it. Structure and hierarchy impede effective communication (overlooked signals, people silenced, dissenting views not welcome). Foresight demands that managers *encourage* worst-case scenario discussions.
- Wishful thinking (desire for positive outcome in terms of cost and schedule) can override a system's fundamental requirements (e.g., specifications) and compromise rational/critical thought. Be *aware* when it has you in its grip.
- Defer to the expertise of your technical *experts* over allegiance to bureaucratic norms (cost or task efficiency, chain of command, procedure, following the rules, going by the book, respect for hierarchy).

Now for a look at an organization which is legendary in its focus on the social aspect of organization, and at which such prescriptions are already well-in-place: Southwest Airlines.

Taking the Social Aspects Perspective Seriously: Southwest Airlines as a Positive Case Study

It would be hard to imagine that the single most profitable publicly-traded company from 1973 to 2003 is an airline. Through the vicissitudes of rising energy costs, multiple bankruptcies in the industry, increased health care costs, and even the terrorist attacks of September 11th, Southwest has remained profitable. It has been the *only* U.S. airline to be profitable *every year of its existence,* 34 consecutive years. It is no small wonder that it regularly earns accolades as one of the world's most admired companies. It is also a regular winner in *Fortune* magazine's annual survey of the "Best Places to Work." There is a connection. Herb Kelleher, the legendary co-founder and Chairman of Southwest, puts it simply when he explains "We have always felt that a company is much stronger if it is bound together by love, rather than by fear." (Charthouse Learning, 2001). Rita Bailey, former Director of Southwest Airlines' University puts it just as succinctly: "When you put people first, profits follow." (2006; see also Cawood & Bailey, 2006) Their employees—from the rank and file all the way up to their executives—are willing to work longer hours for less pay. Their pilots help clean up the flight cabin on "stop-downs." And here's another surprise: Southwest actually ranks as the most heavily unionized of all major airlines in the United States. Its pilots, flight attendants, dispatchers, mechanics, clerical agents, and ramp/fleet service are all represented by bargaining units, adding up to a workforce that is over 82% union. Its labor-conflict index is the lowest in the industry, and it comes to agreement with its bargaining units in the shortest amount of time (Gittell, 2003: pp. 168-169).

Another "secret" in Southwest's success is its willingness to "hire for attitude and train for skill." They hire—and train—for relational competence. (Gittell, 2003). They do not hire egos, but go with a profile of people whose natural inclination is to serve. Kelleher explains, "The people at Southwest derive great pleasure from serving others, because that's what's in their hearts to do." (Charthouse Learning, 2001).

When the World Trade Center towers were engulfed in flames on September 11, 2001, the leadership at Southwest anticipated their 30,000+ employees' concerns: Would they be laid off? Immediately, Herb Kelleher and the top vice presidents (VP) caucused and announced within hours that no one would be laid off, that Southwest would sell off equipment (airplanes) before they let anybody in their "family" go and that the top three executives would take a voluntary pay-cut and work for free, through January 1. Incredibly, employees at Southwest began to volunteer part of *their* salary, too, to help guide the carrier through these troubled times, and management had to—get this!—eventually declare a cap to the giving. And the loyalty extended to Southwest's customers as well. Many passengers who were offered refunds on already-booked flights which had to be cancelled in the following weeks volunteered to let Southwest keep their money. (Bailey, 2006)

Southwest takes the Social Aspects Perspective to heart. It de-emphasizes hierarchy, titles, and bureaucracy. It emphasizes developing people, shared purpose, and "relational coordination." (Gittell, 2003) Utilizing frequent, timely, and open/honest communication, the airline shares information freely. They put the power of shared goals (vision), shared knowledge, and mutual respect to work for a common purpose: "We treat our employee as our number one customer. If they are happy, they will make our customers happy. How is someone who is not happy going to be able to provide exceptional service to others? It's so simple that no one gets it!" laughs Colleen Barrett (Charthouse Learning, 2001), the airline's President who has been with "Herb" from the start. Even their mission statement is full of surprises that thoroughly reflect the embodiment of the Social Aspects of Organization. References to customers and employees are capitalized, and there is *no mention* of their primary activity: flying airplanes! Evidently for this exemplar of people-driven profit-making enterprise, even business is more a "way of being" than a way of doing.

Our Mission
The mission of Southwest Airlines is dedication to the highest quality of Customer Service delivered with a sense of warmth, friendliness, individual pride, and Company Spirit.

To Our Employees
We are committed to provide our Employees a stable work environment with equal opportunity for learning and personal growth. Creativity and innovation are encouraged for improving the effectiveness of Southwest Airlines. Above all, Employees will be provided with the same concern, respect, and caring attitude within the organization that they are expected to share externally with every Southwest Customer. (southwest.com, 2006)

***

Summary

In this chapter, we have elaborated upon the Social Aspects of Organization, reviewing its historical place in the literature. We began with a look back at Douglas McGregor's 50-year old treatise on "The Human Side of Enterprise," to identify core factors relating to human needs that remain salient today. Building on the premise that organizations exist to serve human needs, the core characteristics and processes of organizations were briefly reviewed. These included balancing autonomy with community, differentiation with homogenization, and stability with change. The key drivers of organizations from a social perspective were identified: (1) Awareness of self, others, and your environment (the role of emotional intelligence); (2) Focus on relationships; and (3) Service as the core purpose of individual and organizational endeavor.

The model of servant-leadership was presented as one that is uniquely attuned to the drivers of the Social Aspects Perspective. An extensive articulation of the consequences of neglecting—and attending to—the human side of organization was presented (Table 4-1), along with an analysis of positive and negative consequences associated with viewing organizations from this perspective. We devoted particular attention to the implications of the social perspective for "creating the future we desire," distinguishing between management and leadership and their relationship to understanding root causes of behavior. We noted that our leverage for positive impact increases as we move from surface level events, to discernible patterns, to underlying systemic structures, to mental models and vision.

To demonstrate the applicability of the model, we closed with case study illustrations of NASA (Challenger and Columbia failures) and Southwest Airlines, as examples of organizations which either failed—or succeeded—in taking the social aspects of organization seriously.

The next chapter will discuss the political environment of SPELIT.

***

Bibliography

Chris Argyris. *Personality and Organization.* New York: HarperCollins. 1957.

——— & Donald Schoen. *Theory in Practice: Increasing Professional Effectiveness.* San Francisco: Jossey-Bass. 1974.

Rita Bailey. Personal communication. June 12, 2006.

Scott Cawood & Rita Bailey. *Destination Profit: Creating People-Profit Opportunities in Your Organization.* Mountain View, CA: Davies-Black. 2006.

Ken Blanchard & Michael O'Connor. *Managing by Values.* San Francisco: Berrett-Koehler. 1997.

Ken Blanchard & Norman Vincent Peale. *The Power of Ethical Management.* NY: William Morrow. 1988.

Peter Block. *The Empowered Manager: Positive Political Skills at Work.* San Francisco: Jossey-Bass. 1987.

—–-. *Stewardship: Choosing Service Over Self-Interest.* SF: Berrett-Koehler. 1993.

Lee Bolman & Terrence Deal. *Leading with Soul (Revised Edition).* SF: Jossey-Bass. 2001.

———-. *Reframing Organizations: Artistry, Choice & Leadership.* (2e) SF: Jossey-Bass. 1997.

Kevin Cashman. *Leadership From the Inside Out.* Provo: Executive Excellence. 1998.

Charthouse Learning. *It's So Simple: Inspired by Southwest Airlines.* (DVD). Burnsville, MN. 2001.

Jim Collins. *Good to Great: Why Some Companies Make the Leap...and Others Don't.* New York: Harper-Collins. 2001.

Jim Collins & Jerry Porras. *Built to Last: Successful Habits of Visionary Companies.* New York: HarperCollins. 1997.

—–-. "Level 5 Leadership: The Triumph of Humility and Fierce Resolve." *Harvard Business Review.* January 2001: 67-76.

The Columbia Accident Investigation Board Report. Washington, D.C.: US Government Printing Office. 2003.

Stephen Covey. *Principle-Centered Leadership.* New York: Fireside. 1991.

Henri Fayol. *General and Industrial Management.* Trans. C. Storrs. London: Pittman. 1916.

Mary Parker Follett. "The Giving of Orders." 1926. pp. 152-157 in

Shafritz & Ott, *Classics of Organization Theory (5e)*. Belmont, CA: Wadsworth. 2001

Don Frick & Larry Spears. *The Private Writings of Robert K. Greenleaf: On Becoming a Servant-Leader.* San Francisco: Jossey-Bass. 1996.

Jody Gittell. *The Southwest Airlines Way: Using the Power of Relationships to Achieve High Performance.* New York: McGraw-Hill. 2003.

Daniel Goleman. *Emotional Intelligence.* New York: Bantam: 1995.

———. *Working with Emotional Intelligence.* New York: Bantam. 1998.

Robert Greenleaf. *The Servant as Leader.* Indianapolis: The Greenleaf Center. 1991.

Sue Annis Hammond. *The Thin Book of Appreciative Inquiry (2e).* Bend, OR: Thin Book Publishing. 1998.

Sally Helgesen. *The Female Advantage: Women's Ways of Leadership.* New York: Doubleday. 1990.

Laurel Johnson. *From Mechanistic to Social Systemic Thinking: A Digest of a Talk by Russell L. Ackoff.* Waltham, MA: Pegasus Communications. 1997.

Ronald Heifetz & Marty Linsky. *Leadership on the Line: Staying Alive Through the Dangers of Leading.* Boston: Harvard. 2002.

Daniel Kim. "Foresight as the Central Ethic of Leadership." *Voices of Servant Leadership Series, Vol. 8.* Indianapolis, IN: Greenleaf Center. 2002.

Eric Klein. *You Are the Leader You've Been Waiting For: Enjoying High Performance and High Fulfillment at Work.* Encinitas, CA: Wisdom Heart Press. 2006.

Roger Lewin & Birute Regine. *The Soul at Work: Embracing Complexity Science for Business Success.* New York: Simon & Schuster. 2000.

Mark Maier. "Preparing Managers for the 21st Century: Perspectives on Contemporary Leadership Education." *Journal of Management Systems,* 10 (2): 1-12. Winter 1998.

―――"A Major Malfunction..." The Story Behind the Space Shuttle Challenger Disaster. Video documentary. Albany: State University of New York Research Foundation. 1992.

Abraham Maslow. "Á Theory of Human Motivation" *Psychological Review* 50: p. 370-396. 1943.

Douglas McGregor. "The Human Side of Enterprise." 1957. pp. 179-184 in Shafritz & Ott,*Classics of Organization Theory (5e)*. 2001.

Robert K. Merton. *Social Theory and Social Structure*. Boston: Free Press. 1957.

Barry Oshry. *Seeing Systems: Unlocking the Mysteries of Organizational Life*. San Francisco: Berrett-Koehler. 1995.

―――. *Leading Systems*. San Francisco: Berrett-Koehler. 1999.

Joseph Rost. *Leadership for the 21st Century*. Westport, CT: Praeger. 1991.

Donald Schoen. *The Reflective Practitioner*. New York: Basic. 1983.

Peter Senge. *The Fifth Discipline*. NY: Doubleday. 1990.

Peter Senge, Richard Ross, Bryan Smith, Charlotte Roberts &Art Kleiner. *The Fifth Discipline Fieldbook*. NY: Doubleday. 1994.

Jay Shafritz & Steven Ott. *Classics of Organization Theory (5e)*. Belmont, CA: Wadsworth. 2001.

http://www.southwest.com. Southwest Airlines Website. June 30, 2006.

Frederick W. Taylor. *The Principles of Scientific Management*. New York: Horton. 1911.

Max Weber. *From Max Weber: Essays in Sociology*. Edited and translated by H.H. Gerth & C. Wright Mills, eds. Oxford: Oxford University Press. 1946.

Margaret Wheatley & Myron Kellner-Rogers. *A Simpler Way*. San Francisco: Berrett-Koehler. 1996.

Ken Wilber. *A Theory of Everything: An Integral Vision for Business, Politics, Science, and Spirituality.* Boston: Shambhala. 2000.

Chapter 5
Exploring the Political Frame

Dr. June Schmieder-Ramirez
Michael A. Moodian
Pepperdine University

***

Introduction

The political analysis framework can be viewed as how an organization deals with competing interests, views, assumptions, and values. Our society does accommodate many different political viewpoints, but occasionally there are "shifts in the tectonic plates" that set off major debate. For example in today's newspaper there are articles regarding the debate between supporting American made automobiles or purchasing Asian brands. It is important to gather all information about this debate as many Asian based companies hire American workers. However, this is a political debate that is ongoing.

The purpose of this chapter is to address the importance of the political component in the SPELIT POWER MATRIX and illustrate how a leader can track the political issues in the organization and be able to tease out the driving forces from the restraining forces within the organization. The first part of the chapter deals with definitions that include leadership, power, relationships, internal, and external political forces. The chapter ends with examples of how a leader might use SPELIT to analyze the political dynamics with an organization.

***

Political Thought

In order to understand the foundation of political thought, it is necessary to read the political philosophies of Rawls, Kant, Rousseau, Aristotle and Plato. All have strong views on the nature of mankind and the political state. The rise of political thought can be traced to over 6000 B.C. with the rise of the city-states and the formation of craftsmen and guilds. This is the time of the beginning of the social strata that we have today. However, to analyze a modern organization, you should not only look at the organizational chart but look at who has access to resources within the organization. The reporting arrangements are also important. The questions of power including *reward power* (the power of achieving financial or other types of gains), *legitimate power* (the power of authority), *referent power* (those who are close to persons of authority), *expert power* (leading from experience or education), and *incentive or coercive power* are also important to assess (Robbins, 2005). Tubbs (2007) and Pierce and Newstrom (2000) detail these 5 specific types of power and their application within an organization. Table 5-1 outlines the 5 types and provides examples of how each are practiced in organizational settings. Though everyone has experienced interactions with others who have exerted the types of power described above, the concept of power is often not analyzed systematically as it is in this table (Tubbs, 2007).

Table 5-1
Five Specific Types of Power

Power Type	Example
Reward Power	Promotions and raises
Coercive Power	Punishment, enforcement of rules
Legitimate Power	Influence of elected official
Referent Power	Personal identification
Expert Power	Respect of one's expertise

In order to understand the political inner workings of an organization, one might read Hirschhorn's (1993) text, *the Psychodynamics of Organizations*. In the text various firms are analyzed, including a law firm, to observe the dynamics of social and political activity. In Block's (1987) *The Empowered Manager*, political dynamics within an organizational setting are demonstrated by an ability for a leader to maintain her own position while potentially minimizing resistance from others within the organization.

Definitions and Key Terms

As we explore the political frame in SPELIT we are also describing how one views power, talks about power, and uses power to gain some end. A dichotomy of power is presented in Table 5-2.

Table 5-2
Old and New Views of Power Showing Dichotomy in Politics

Old View of Power	New View of Power
Hierarchical	Organization chart but fluid at the end
Who reports to whom	Expertise at lower level
Glass Ceiling	Loosening up of glass ceiling
Inconsistent human resource systems	Human resource systems consistent with legal system
Power in coalitions	Power in coalitions
Power tactics differ by culture	Power tactics differ by culture
Location of power hierarchical	Power can reside in any level of Organization

Leadership

The use of the political frame of the SPELIT model can be very powerful. When one has employees gather and discuss the restraining forces and enabling forces, one of the most obvious ways to enable a plan or goal is to "grease the wheels" politically. There is no more powerful way to enable a plan to come to fruition than to convince the leader that this plan can be accomplished. Leaders achieve their goals, while power is the means for them to achieve it. Perceptive leaders might use the SPELIT model to accomplish their goals because the model is effective in analyzing the present situation. Leaders keep the vision before the group while the political frame can help the leader accomplish his or her goals.

It has been commonly said that "politics equals power" and that gaining political power is a key competency to achieving success within an organization. In politics, "the power balance is in constant flux" (Davidson & Oleszek, 2006, p. 330). Understanding the political dynamics of an organization can be fundamental in accurately assessing the organization before, for example, a transition or change initiative. When two companies experience a merger, the dynamics of power shift. Those who previously held political power over the members of a company change. Senior-level executives from one company may now hold positions within the other, consequently changing the power dynamics for such employees as well. Positions shifted through such a merger lead to new relationships and new leadership dynamics.

Relationships

The leader uses the political frame to analyze the political relationships within the organization. Depending upon the type of organization, relationships can make a huge difference in success. Many a leader has "gone down in flames" because of an alienation that occurs in relationships within the organization. This strand of the SPELIT model ties very closely with the intercultural strand. Understanding cultures, small group dynamics, and how employees relate to each other is key to having a successful organization. Sun Tzu said of analyzing military might:

> Which ruler has the Tao? Which general has greater ability? Who has gained the advantages of Heaven and Earth? Whose laws and order are more thoroughly implemented? Whose forces are stronger? Whose officers and troops are better trained? Whose rewards and punishments are clearer? From these I will know victory and defeat! (p. 69)

The descriptors by Sun Tzu are just as relevant today as they were in his time. The more organized the "troops" are in an organization and the more that certain values are espoused together, the more successful that organization is. The question may arise as to where such political power comes from. One notion may be that it stems from the communication system or division of labor within an organization (Pfeffer, 1992).

Internal and External Political Forces

The political frame of the SPELIT model can analyze both the internal and external forces of the organization. As noted in an earlier chapter, the Butterfield Fabric Company was producing fabric that was not the fabric of choice in the external environment. Internally, its employees were not prepared for change. Therefore the company was on a downward spiral to failure. It was only when the employees were brought together to determine group direction was any progress made. The employees determined the driving forces that were helping the company and the driving forces that were hurting the company. As Pfeffer (1981) adds, "Power affects the allocation of resources both across departments and across personnel categories. Power affects the succession of executives in organizations as well as the promotion of persons at all organizational levels" (pp. 231–232).

How SPELIT Might be Utilized from a Political Point of View in an Organization: Southwest Airlines

If a leader wished to closely observe the political dynamics of a company, it is recommended that the political frame be selected and viewed from many different angles. One could look at the political driving forces, for example, that impact an organization. Additionally, one could just review the political/relational strand of the organization. Table 5-3 shows how it would be possible to select goals from an organization and review with the employees the constraining forces and the driving forces towards completing that goal.

Table 5-3
Southwest Airlines Political Model Constraining and Driving Forces

Goals	Constraining Forces	Driving Forces
Goal #1: Maintain Effective Relationships	Size of company	Engrained in culture
Goal #2: Effective Communication	Complexity and size of teams at departure gate	Culture encourages communication
Goal #3: Be a team player	Some employees may not have this attitude?	Desire to be part of a team

Another Example of the Utilization of SPELIT from a Political Point of View

To demonstrate another example, let's discuss a potential merger of two companies referred to earlier in this chapter. For this example, one company if a Fortune 500 food and beverage manufacturer (Company A). The other is a smaller privately held beverage manufacturer that posted net sales of more than $150 million the previous year (Company B). When conducting a SPELIT analysis, the political drivers are diverse. Because Company B may represent less of an institutionalized environment than Company A, employees in Company B may have to make adjustments from new types of power, as communication may have been multidirectional versus top-down (Fischer, Mazur & Moodian, 2004). This process could lead to a greater feeling of empowerment among the members of the staff, therefore leading to a higher performing organization (Tubbs, 2006). Simultaneously, given the enormous size of Company A, it likely invests tremendously in its government lobbying efforts. The members of Company B may now likely be exposed to more corporate communications initiatives that they may not necessarily be accustomed to in an effort to align them toward their particular position or stance (Herrnson, Shaiko, & Wilcox, 2005). An outline of the political drivers for such a merger is displayed in Table 5-4.

Table 5-4
Political Drivers for Hypothetical Company Merger

Driver	Driving Force 1	Driving Force 2	Driving Force 3
Political	Those with political power would now change; some may have experienced fear because of a loss of power.	The transition to less of an institutionalized environment may have meant less top-down communication.	Company A may have administered corporate communications campaigns to align new employees with lobbying efforts that they support.

An important consideration when examining the power dynamic comes from Greene (2000) who states in *The 48 Laws of Power*:

> [O]n the day-to-day level people are creatures of habit. Too much innovation is traumatic and will lead to revolt. If you are new to a position of power, or an outsider trying to build a power base, make a show of respecting the old ways of doing things. If change is necessary, make it feel like a gentle improvement on the past. (p. 392)

Such a statement would be important to convey to those with power within Company A. Based on this, slow gradual change would be the recommended philosophy throughout the undertaking versus sudden and abrupt change (Bridges, 2003).

***

Summary

Acclaimed physicist Albert Einstein once stated, "Politics is more difficult than physics" (as cited in Reardon, 2005, p. 2). The effective leader is very cognizant of the importance of mastering such difficulties inherent in the political scene both within and outside of the organization. Such a scene is constantly evolving, and could potentially catch a CEO or other prominent leader off guard. The SPELIT POWER MATRIX helps to keep the leader informed and cognizant of the increasingly evolving aspects of politics and power so that a complete and thorough analysis can be accomplished.

The next chapter will discuss the drivers of the economic environment of the SPELIT methodology.

***

References

Block, P. (1987). *The empowered manager: Positive political skills at work*. San Francisco: Jossey-Bass.

Bridges, W. (2003). *Managing transitions* (2nd ed.). Cambridge, MA: Da Capo Press.

Davidson, R. H., & Oleszek, W. J. (2006). *Congress and its members* (10th ed.). Washington, DC: CQ Press.

Fischer, C., Mazur, G., & Moodian, M. (2004). 21st century leadership and its intersection with organizational culture. *Scholar and Educator: The Journal of the Society of Educators and Scholars, 26*(1), 44–56.

Herrnson, P. S., Shaiko, R. G., & Wilcox, C. (2005). *The interest group connection: Electioneering, lobbying and policy making in Washington* (2nd ed.). Washington DC: CQ Press.

Hirschhorn, L. (1993). The workplace within: The psychodynamics of the organization. MIT Press. Boston: MA

Greene, R. (2000). *The 48 laws of power.* New York: Penguin Books.

Pierce, J.L., & Newstrom, J.W. (2000). *Leaders and the leadership process (2nd ed.).* New York: McGraw Hill.

Pfeffer, J. (1992). *Managing with power: Politics and influence in organizations.* Boston: Harvard Business School Press.

Pfeffer, J. (1981). *Power in organizations.* Cambridge, MA: Ballinger Publishing Company.

Reardon, K. (2005). *It's all politics: Winning in a world where hard work and talent aren't enough.* New York: Currency.

Robbins, S. P. (2005). *Essentials of organizational behavior* (8th ed.). Upper Saddle River, NJ: Pearson Prentice Hall.

Sun Tzu, (1994) The art of war. New York: Barnes and Noble Press.

Tubbs, S. L. (2007). *A systems approach to small group interaction.* Boston: McGraw Hill.

Chapter 6
Assessment of the Economic Environment

Elizabeth Martin and Dr. Michael Lacourse

***

Introduction

The SPELIT environmental analysis technique includes a comprehensive assessment of the economic conditions affecting the operation and outcomes of an educational organization. In this analytic model, the economic condition of the organization is defined as those factors that affect the production and consumption of resources needed to operate the organization. The comprehensive assessment of existing economic conditions will therefore require an exhaustive evaluation of the organizations current and projected assets, revenues, and expenditures.

For example, macroeconomic factors that most significantly impact student access to education, such as government funding and student aid, receive the greatest attention among higher education finance and policy experts because of their broad impact on higher education effectiveness. These factors are controlled mainly by state legislatures and federal agencies and define the financial framework for most institutions, primarily public higher education, to achieve sustained educational effectiveness. While these macro-economic factors must be considered as an essential component within any organizational economic assessment, the assessment of institutional finance and budgets are the focus of this chapter because they more directly impact programmatic quality and can be influenced locally through interventions derived from thoughtful strategic planning.

Though bound by academic traditions and governmental oversight that tends to limit university assets and revenues to those that are tangible, such as student tuition and state general funds, a growing number of educational institutions are successfully leveraging their intangible assets to both complement their tangible assets and buffer against cyclical variations in state budgets. Examples include fee-for-service activities, corporate sponsorship, executive education programs, intellectual property contracts, and for-profit enterprises operated through foundations. In addition to the accumulation of assets, intangible assets such as intellectual capital may be used to improve the management of risk and administrative processes. Educational organizations also possess an extraordinary pool of intellectual capital that heretofore has been used only sparingly to produce additional resources. The comprehensive economic assessment of institutional assets within the SPELIT model includes an evaluation of both current and potential tangible and intangible assets as well as expenditures.

Formal accounting systems employed by most organizations define tangible assets as cash, inventory, investments, receivables (e.g., student tuition and state general funds), and property and equipment. Less recognizable, but increasingly important in an information-based organization, are the intangible assets such as quality of management, customer (student/alumni) loyalty, information infrastructure, operational secrets, patents, goodwill, intellectual capital, and research activity. A complete assessment of economic conditions must include an analysis of current tangible and intangible resources as well as projected resources. The following is a brief overview of the different classes of revenue and expenditures that are evaluated within the economic environmental assessment.

***

Assessment of Revenue Sources

The financing of higher education relies primarily on state funding, student tuition, or both. In public colleges and universities, these two revenues sources are commingled centrally, and campus units receive a single allocation. In private institutions, resource allocation to campus units co-mingles student tuition with other revenue sources (see Table 6-1). If an assessment of these revenue sources is being conducted at the university level, appropriate data may be obtained from the funding multiplier used by the state and enrollment reports. If the assessment is being conducted at the campus unit level, there is likely a different multiplier that may be based on student enrollment, faculty allocation, research activity, program type, or other funding factors. This multiplier can be used in the economic assessment to create "what-if" scenarios that will predict funding levels based on one or more of the determining factors. The assessment should further consider anticipated changes due to budget reductions, budget expansions, or changing enrollments.

Table 6-1
Resource and Expense Categories to be Included in the Economic Assessment

Resource Categories	Expense Categories
Student Tuition	Human Resources (salary, benefits, search and selection, training)
State Funding	Administration and Operations
Charitable Contributions/Philanthropy	Maintenance, Upgrade, and Repair (MUR)
Corporate Sponsorship	Capital Projects
Fee-for-Service Activity	Investment
Buildings and Capital Goods	Equipment, Repair and Maintenance
Grants and Contracts	
Intellectual Capital	

Assessment of Philanthropy and Corporate Sponsorship

An increasing tangible resource for both public and private higher education is corporate and individual philanthropy. Educational philanthropy is the voluntary act of donating money, goods, or other service to support an educational institution, often over an extended period of time. A related source of funding is charitable giving, with the former being more closely aligned with wealthy contributors and the latter associated with more modest contributions by a larger number of people. Charitable funds are solicited from individuals, organizations/

foundations, and corporations. Data concerning assets and revenues derived through philanthropic or charitable activity is most often available from the institution's affiliated 501(c)(3) foundation. Reports of the prior year's activity are typically published annually and can be used a primary data source for the assessment. Other sources of data for the assessment can be obtained from the university office of development/advancement, where data concerning fund raising targets, trends, and future expectations are stored.

Beyond philanthropy and charitable giving, many educational institutions are adopting strategies for leveraging their intangible assets to create partnerships with corporate and foundation sponsors. These partnerships afford the production of new tangible assets such as buildings and other capital projects, as well as new intangible assets such as instructional and academic support programs and endowed chairs. The assessment of current sponsorship activity can be completed by accessing financial reports from the office of development/ advancement or from an appropriate financial office. An assessment of future or potential sponsorship opportunity will require a more detailed analysis of the political and legal environment to establish institutional constraints on sponsorship activity as well as a separate market analysis to construct an inventory of sponsorship opportunities.

Assessment of Grant and Contract Activity

Although the majority of grant and contract funding awarded to educational institutions is earmarked for direct project-related expenses, most granting agencies and contracting organizations pay indirect funds to the institution that are often used to supplement operating budgets or capital projects. The assessment of current grant and contract activity can usually be obtained from the affiliated foundation, where the funds are typically administered. The assessment of future grant and contract activity is difficult because the nature of the award process is competitive and there is no way to determine the likelihood of an award being granted. The assessment could, however, examine the various sources of grants and contracts that may be accessible by the organization and determine whether it is feasible to pursue the funding.

Assessment of Buildings and Other Capital Goods

The assessment of buildings and other capital goods as a component of the organization's economic condition is both necessary and prudent, as these tangible assets may be used to accumulate additional resources. For example, existing buildings and grounds might be rented to off-campus groups in return for fees or in-kind donations. Specialized facilities (e.g., computer laboratories) could command even higher rental fees that could be used to support the ongoing maintenance, upgrade, and repair of the lab.

The assessment of buildings and capital goods as a potential source of revenues requires a more formal market analysis and associated business plan. For example, what is the market for the type of facility you wish to make available to the public? If there is a wide market and little competition, the assessment would conclude that there is the potential to generate greater revenues than if the market was small and there are many competitors.

Another perspective on the assessment of buildings and capital goods is to ask whether those buildings or goods could be shared by multiple users within the same organization, thereby reducing the redundant purchase of new goods. Savings from the elimination of redundancy would itself lead to increased mission-critical resources.

Assessment of Fee-for-Service Activity

Educational institutions are increasingly dependent on fee-for-service activities, such as research centers, clinics, facility rental, executive/continuing education, events, camps, real estate development, catering and hotel management, corporate technology parks and many others. In some instances, these non-traditional resources contribute significant revenues to operational budgets or the advancement of the institutional endowment. While larger projects often generate resources that are directed towards general institutional budgets, in some cases fee-for-service activities are operated by individual campus units. An assessment of these activities includes both the recognition of current fee-for-service activities, their financial benefits to the organization, and potential for economic growth.

Assessment of Intellectual Capital

Also included in the economic assessment is an evaluation of the organization's intangible assets, such as intellectual capital, that could supply leverage to reduce costs or pursue additional assets and resources. Intellectual capital makes an organization worth more than its assets. The management of intellectual capital involves the utilization of knowledge, collaboration, and process-engagement to make decisions and take actions that lead to cost reductions, productivity increases, or the creation of new resources. The assessment of intellectual capital as a source of cost reduction and revenue/asset production will require the analysis of personnel and processes. For example, what are the qualifications and skill sets of the employees and could those employees be assigned to tasks that produce new resources or reduce costs?

The highly trained work force found in the modern university represents an unequalled source of intellectual capital that has traditionally been underutilized in the production of both tangible and intangible resources for the university. Tenure-track faculty are hired primarily to teach, conduct research, and provide service to the university and community, and not to produce new financial resources. The exception to this rule is that some research-centered universities expect faculty to produce resources in order to achieve tenure and promotion. Few faculty contracts, however, include job responsibilities that lead to the creation of new university resources.

A new partnership-centered model of higher education seeks opportunities to create new or expand existing relationships with external organizations, such as corporations, agencies, and foundations. Institutions of higher learning employ a faculty with expertise that transcends much of the social and economic spectrum, offering many opportunities for partnerships that could lead to the production of new resources. An assessment of these opportunities should be included in the economic environmental analysis.

***

Assessment of Expenditures

The expenditures required to successfully operate an educational organization represents the other half of the economic environmental assessment. While the assessment of assets and revenues will determine the resources available for consumption by the organization, the assessment of expenditures supplies critical information about what resources are needed to achieve the organizational mission. The balance of funds in these categories must be achieved to operate the organization. Expenditure categories include human resources, administration and operations, maintenance, upgrade and repair maintained, upgraded, and repaired (MUR), capital projects, and investment. Although budgeting investment costs in an educational organization is atypical, we will include them here because of our belief that a successful organization must invest a portion of its resources into long-term growth and development. Within each expenditure category, expenses can be further categorized as recurring or non-recurring.

Assessment of Human Resources Expenditures

The largest expense category in higher education is faculty and staff salaries, benefits, and support services. This category includes costs associated with faculty and staff hiring and training. The assessment of current and projected costs for personnel requires access to salary and benefits data and well as data concerning hiring and training costs. The data about current costs may be obtained from the organization's fiscal officers. An assessment of future costs should include anticipated cost of living increases, savings associated with expected retirements, costs of replacement personnel, new hiring to meet changing enrollment needs, as well as sabbaticals and other personnel absences.

Assessment of Administrative and Operational Expenditures

The costs for administering and operating an academic organization will vary across units and levels within the organizational hierarchy. For example, the administration and operation costs of the office of student services will be very different from the costs to operate a political science department, which will be different than the costs for operating a department of engineering. The expenses in this category includes utilities, office supplies, printing costs, janitorial supplies, technology, communications, travel, small equipment purchases, instructional supplies, special events, and other organization-specific expenditures. Most of these costs are recurring, so an organization should able to readily supply the information necessary to complete this part of the assessment. Non-recurring operational costs may be needed to support one time events or small capital projects in support of operations.

Assessment of MUR Expenditures

Buildings, grounds, and equipment must be maintained, upgraded, and repaired (MUR) on a regular basis to ensure that services and resources needed to operate the organization are uninterrupted. These costs can vary widely across organizations and are determined by the size and type of organization. These costs must be included in the assessment of expenditures needed to operate the organization and may be both recurring and non-recurring. The assessment of these costs is an ongoing concern, with a designated person responsible for the inventory of equipment and buildings and a plan for maintaining equipment and buildings. The organization should assume that these expenses must be included in their budget. In some cases, MUR is a recurring expense with a predictable and consistent cost structure that is applied to a list of MUR projects needing to be completed. In other instances, where the cost of MUR may be large, there may need to be a large sum of money earmarked for a project that would be a one-time or non-recurring expense.

Assessment of Capital Expenditures

Not part of the general operating budget, the capital budget refers to the expenditures associated with capital improvement such as constructing or renovating buildings, purchasing new automated systems, or other major expenditures that have a multi-year lifetime. Capital funds can also be used to acquire land and property, pay for consultants, architectural services, furnishings, and equipment. In public institutions, capital budgets are often funded by special referenda, while in private institutions capital projects are funded through donations. Capital projects can sometimes be funded through budget transfers internally and budgets can be carried across fiscal years, whereas the operating budget cannot. Capital funds are normally invested until used. Capital projects are major expenditures that are usually spread over several years; the time it takes to collect the funds, plan the project, implement and complete the project. Within an educational institution, the capital project must be included in the master plan.

The assessment of costs associated with capital projects is determined through a needs assessment, followed by an estimate of costs to achieve the needs. Once the costs have been established and a budget agreed upon, the capital funds are solicited either through the state in the case of a public institution or through donors in the case of a private institution. Increasingly, public institutions are seeking capital funds from private donors as well.

Assessment of Investment Expenditures

The final expense category to include in the economic environment assessment is investment costs. This category includes those costs that are necessary to stimulate growth and development within the organization. Examples of expenses would be the purchase of new research or instructional equipment, hiring of consultants or temporary staff to coordinate or conduct a project, and funds to support time for faculty to engage in program development. Some organizations plan for investment by including it as recurring expense, with annual expenses determined by a prioritization process that emerges from the organization's strategic plan. Other organizations do not include investment as a recurring expense, but invest only when extra funds become available due to cost-savings or when nonrecurring resources become available. The allocation of resources for investment opportunity is a strategic decision and the assessment of associated costs requires an analysis of the organization's existing strategic plan, as well as an analysis of emerging opportunities that have been identified by the leadership team.

***

Summary

The accumulation and consumption of resources is an essential activity of an organization in achieving its mission and requires thoughtful planning. This chapter presented a description of how the economic conditions of an organization must be assessed as a component of the SPELIT environmental analysis technique. The analysis of the economic conditions must be considered within the context of the social, political, legal, intercultural, and technological environments that are defined in the accompanying chapters. The assessment of costs and expenditures is a dynamic process, where the estimated expenditures are used to determine the needed resources, while the availability of resources constraints the expenditures. Planners must achieve this delicate balance, while simultaneously working within the constraints determined by the other SPELIT factors. Collecting information about the current economic condition of an organization involves the gathering of data from the organization's fiscal officer. Although time consuming to collect and review, these data are much more readily available than the data needed to project future production and consumption. The information needed to complete an assessment of future conditions is gathered from various sources both within and outside the organization and must be done in consideration of the information gathered from the other components of the SPELIT environmental analysis. The assessment of economic conditions should proceed with the goal of maximizing the organizational outcomes. Consequently, the assessor searches for opportunities to reduce costs and accumulate resources. In achieving both of these goals, the organization will reap the benefit of improving the quality of its outcomes or expanding the number of outcomes.

***

References

Bingham, R.D., Hill, E.W., White, S.B., (1990), Financing Economic Development, Sage Publications.

Lipsey, R.G., Steiner, P.O., Douglas, D.P., (1994), Economics, Harper & Row, Publishers, New York.

Matzer, J. Jr., (1994), Capital Projects: New Strategies for Planning, Management, and Finance

Zumeta, W., (2001), Higher Education Finance in the Nineties, *Lessons for the New Millennium,* The NEA 2001 Almanac of Higher Education.

Chapter 7
Assessing the Legal Environment In the SPELIT POWER MATRIX

John C. Tobin, J.D.
Pepperdine University
Graduate School of Education and Psychology

***

Introduction

The legal element of the SPELIT POWER MATRIX is significant, because it helps us to address what is "codified" in an organization. Those procedures and policies can help us to determine the internal culture and therefore know "where we are" and how our decisions as leaders impact the internal and external environments. Our assessment of the legal portion of the environment can be key. For example, laws that facilitate the entry and continuity of employment for the handicapped in the United States have significantly affected the way buildings, workplaces and workflow are designed and effectuated. Laws which regulate the manner in which gender may serve as a selection factor in hiring and promotion has radically modified the role of women in the United States workforce over the last fifty years. Therefore, the knowledge of policies and procedures in systems are key to our efficacy as leaders.

In order to better describe the legal environment or domain of the organization, this chapter first examines the greater environment of the law, what theories explain the source and authority for the law, and what are the mechanisms for enforcing the law. With these elements as a basis for analysis, we next consider the change agents available to the organization within the legal domain. Finally, we examine how the organization operates when located within the jurisdiction of various legal enforcement issues.

SPELIT asks, "What is the legal domain of an organization's environment?" To obtain a more precise view, we might ask, what is the environment of the law? The law is defined as follows:

> a rule or mode of conduct or action that is prescribed or formally recognized as binding by a supreme controlling authority or is made obligatory by a sanction (as an edict, decree, prescript, order, ordinance, statute, resolution, rule, judicial decision, or usage) made, recognized, or enforced by the controlling authority a rule of conduct or action prescribed or formally recognized as binding or enforced by a controlling authority. Webster's Third New International Dictionary, Unabridged. (2002). Merriam-Webster, 2002. http://unabridged.merriam-webster.com. Retrieved June 2006.

Peeling back this onion-like structure, what is the source or root for this rule or mode? What is the standard against which to measure whether conduct will be prescribed as required or proscribed as forbidden by the community? Here we move back from rules to aspirations, or ethics. Generally, ethics have been appreciated as a society's ongoing determination that a particular mode of conduct is either acceptable or unacceptable. Since societies tend to change over time (Horner, 2004), ethics may be seen as transitory over time.

But the whole purpose of a system of right and wrong is to serve as a talisman over time; thus there must be some fixed signs of right and wrong. Here, we enter the territory of morality. Morals, whether shaped by religious tenet or philosophical precept, are intended to remain as a bellwether over time, and thus, the opposite of transitory. That fixed definition may be called a moral system, one which posits fixed definitions of right and wrong. That this fault line between transitory and fixed is significant will be further illustrated later in our discussion.

In Part 1 of this chapter, we will examine the development of the two key theories of the formation of law: natural law, which is based on a fixed system and legal positivism, which is based on the transitory determination of a body, such as a legislature, which is formally authorized to establish laws. From there we will examine how these theories developed into different systems of enforcement. In Part 2, we will assess how these systems impact the organization and where an organization may find change agents within each system.

***

PART 1. WHAT THEORIES EXPLAIN THE OPERATION OF THE LAW?

In discussing the environment of the law, we noted that ethics were transitory and morals more fixed. Do these two distinctions offer some insight into the manner in which laws are drafted? Let us start with the concept of duty. Generally a duty is an obligation for one party to behave in a specified manner with respect to another. The obligation either stems from a fixed basis, such as a moral system, or a transitory system, such as a community-based code. These distinctions mirror the two major theories of the nature of the law (jurisprudence): natural law and legal positivism. As a working definition let us consider law as the codification of duties owed by persons within a society to one another.

A. Natural Law Theory

The concept of law's function offered by the theory of natural law arises from St. Thomas Aquinas' observation "*lex inuista non est lex*," "unjust law is not law." Thus, a law which promulgates a duty, which is not grounded in morality, is not a duty at all. Here, the fundamental law is to do good and avoid evil. Since good and evil are objective or normative, every law must conform to the original imperative. Any deviation from that imperative renders the law unjust. Paraphrasing Sir William Blackstone, the father of the common law of England and a member of the historical lineage of the American legal system, "no valid law may conflict with the natural law, and all valid laws derive from the natural law." William Blackstone (1823). Commentaries on the law of England. Books 1-4, 1765-1769 (first published 1823, Oxford, Clarendon Press) (Chicago, University of Chicago Press, 1979).

Natural law presumes that man's rational ability, God given, allows humans to rationally conclude that which is good and evil: this is the natural law. In his *Summa Theologiae* (Summary Treatise of Theology, 1265-73) Aquinas asserted that the product of this divinely given rationality was the *eternal law*. This participation in the eternal law by rational creatures is called the natural law. Thus, in medieval times, anything ungodly was manifestly evil. Since the right to govern was divinely given to the King of, in turn, The Holy Roman Empire, France, England, Germany, and Spain, opposition to the King was inherently evil and thus, illegal. The key to the validity of a natural law statute was and is its antecedent in the nature of good and evil. Thus, in paraphrasing St. Thomas Aquinas' statement that an immoral law is not an enforceable law, any statutory provision that does not accord with the unwritten but commonly accepted moral code of a nation is, at the very least, subject to a challenge as to its efficacy.

The American legal system, historically, is rooted in the natural law system. However, waves of statutory or code-based legislation have made the U.S. system more mixed than a true natural law system. For example, consider the case of *U.S. v. Lynch*, 1996 U.S. App. Lexis 32729 (2nd Cir 1996). One litigant sought to validate Aquina's proposition about immoral law. Mr. Lynch, a member of a pro-life, anti-abortionist organization was prosecuted by the federal government under the Freedom of Access to Clinic Entrances Act (FACE), which prohibits the threat or use of force to obstruct the entrance to a reproductive health provider. In seeking the invalidation of the statute, the defendant argued that the FACE statute protected the taking of human life, contrary to any natural or moral formulation of law, and hence was null and void. The Court of Appeals for the Seconds Circuit, upheld Lynch's federal district court's conviction, citing the trail court judge's ruling on the defendant's natural law argument:

> That seal above my head says…this is Caesar's court. This is not a church, this is not a temple, this is not a mosque. And we don't live in a theocracy. This is a court of law. I will look at all the *legal* issues. (p. TBS, emphasis added)

US V. Lynch, at 32734

This case illustrates the turbulence in the long path of development of the law in the United States, which has waxed and waned between natural law (consider the 19th Amendment establishing prohibition as the law of the land) and legal positivism (illustrated by the USSC decision defending the burning of the United States flag as free speech under the 1st Amendment.) The controversy continues today as the several states consider "defense of marriage" amendments to state constitutions, in the shadow of congressional rejection of a defense of marriage amendment to the U.S. constitution.

Another example of a natural law system is that of *shari'a*, the legal and judicial system codified in the holy Muslim book, the Qur'an. This system is said to be practiced in its purest form within the Kingdom of Saudi Arabia and in the Islamic Republic of Iran. Brown, N. (1997) has noted that the Islamic *shari'a* is not an easily identifiable set of rules that can be mechanically applied, but a long and quite varied intellectual tradition. The rule of law in the Arab world is dictated by the Courts in Egypt and the Arab states of the Gulf (Cambridge University Press).).

Many Middle Eastern countries continue to incorporate some traditional *shari'a* into their legal codes, especially in the area of personal-status law, which governs marriage, divorce, and inheritance. In other areas of the law, such as the criminal code, most Islamic nations have attempted to limit the application of traditional *shari'a*, replacing it either with secular legislation or with laws characterized as modern interpretations of *shari'a*. In general, each nation's legal code tends to reflect a variety of historical and cultural influences. For example some Middle Eastern legal codes have their roots in the Napoleonic law system and the Ottoman Empire (Brown, 1997).

Rounding out the discussion of natural law systems, single party states, such as the former Union of Soviet Socialist Republics and the People's Republic of China (at least prior to the economic changes of Chinese Party Secretary Deng Xiaoping in 1982) Marxism-Leninism, and the theory of social realism served as the moral system underpinning the law of those countries. Rather than an independent judiciary serving as a neutral third party for the settling disputes between private persons, the party provided bureaucratic agents who served as both fact finders and decision-makers within strict ideological guidelines. Finally, tribal law systems, such as those seen in segments of Afghanistan, regions in Africa, and in the northern provinces of Pakistan, also illustrate natural law systems.

Theory of Legal Positivism

The polar or conceptual opposite of the natural law system is that of legal positivism. This theory derives from the convergence of the thoughts of two of the great philosophers of the 19th Century, Bentham and Hobbes. Jeremy Bentham (1748-1832), was the British philosopher who founded the doctrine of *utilitarianism*. Sir Thomas Hobbs (1588- 1679) said, "Law, properly, is the word of him, that by right hath command over others." Key to Hobbes notion was that there existed a social contact between man, by which each person's original power is yielded to a sovereign, who regulates conduct. The concept of a sovereign imposing a system for order combines with Bentham's concept of the greatest good for the greatest number in forming the foundation of legal positivism.

More recently, Harvard Law Professor H.L.A. Hart, in *Positivism and the Separation of Law and Morals*" laid out a tripartite architecture for explaining Positivism 71 Harvard Law Review 593 (1958), also see Hart, HLA The Concept of Law Second edition (Oxford, Clarendon Press, 1994.). The three key precepts of legal positivism are:

i. The *social fact thesis* posits that a law is valid is based upon a social fact, in other words, that an authoritative entity within a society formed or promulgated the law. This thesis goes to the source of authority of law;
ii. The *conventionist thesis* posits that the promulgation of the law, the social fact, occurred according to the prescribed procedure of the authority; and,
iii. The *separationist thesis* posits that the validity of the law does not per se, depend on any stated system of morality. Note that this is to be distinguished from the fact that a particular law may have a moral component or relationship to a moral. The key is that the positivist theory of law does not rely on the existence of any particular system of morality.

Thus a duty under legal positivism is a formulation adopted by a recognized authority according to the established rigors of procedure that defines a standard of conduct and the consequences, including any penalty for varying from that standard.

A key example of a legal system based on legal positivism is the the original Napoleonic Code, or *Code Napoléon* (originally called the *Code civil des francais,* or civil code of the French), the French system of laws established at the behest of Napoléon. It entered into force on March 21, 1804. It was based on Roman law and followed Justinian's *Corpus Juris Civilis* in dividing civil law into: 1) personal status, 2) property, and 3) the acquisition of property.

The intention behind the Napoleonic Code was to reform the French legal system in accordance with the principles of the French Revolution. Before the code, France did not have a single set of laws, and the existing ones were rooted in the natural law system which supported the hierarchical, feudal law systems of the day. Premised on the principles of the French Revolution: liberté, equalité, fraternité, the Civil Napoleonic Code rejected the premise of Natural Law and is decidedly positivist. The law is found solely in the statutes, without reference to an external moral or natural law.

Substantive and Procedural Laws

Under natural law or positivism, laws are formulated to address two key areas: substantive laws, which address conduct between parties (public and private) and procedural laws, which address the administration or processing of claims based upon the substantive law. Substantive laws are further divided into specific subject matter areas:

i. Criminal: laws created by the government that impose duties on persons with respect to the public in general, such as to not kill, steal, or engage in other illegal activity;
ii. Civil: laws created by the government (society) which define the duties owed between private parties;
iii. Regulatory: quasi-criminal duties imposed on organizations on the basis of subject matter, such as occupational, environmental, or land-use regulations.

Procedural laws regulate the processing of legal claims or actions through a system for compelling compliance with the law. Such laws may specific who or what entity may file a legal claim or initiate litigation; these laws may set time limits within which an action must be initiated or thereafter considered abandoned. Such laws often control the staging or processing actions from an initial filing stage, through a fact-finding stage, to a decision-making phase, and in some systems, to an appellate or reviewing stage. One group of commentators has suggested that the efficiency of a legal system may be inversely proportionate to the complexity or "formalism" of its procedural legal structure. Djankov et al, 2003, Courts, Quarterly Journal of Economics 118 (2): pp. 493-496.

How Do These Elements of the Legal Domain Effect the Organization?

A. Enforcement as a Measure of Influence on the Organization

A key measure of influence on an organization from forces within the legal domain is the means or the efficacy of enforcing compliance with the law, whatever its source or authority, by a court or other enforcement system. Enforcement systems maybe broken down into those with or without a judicial system (i.e., an independent entity), separate from the law-giving authoritative source, which has co-equal power to interpret and enforce the law. Within systems having a tradition of a judicial system, sometimes called rule of law systems (Miller & Perito, 2004), a further division may be made: common law-adversarial system and civil law-inquisitorial system.

Rule of Law States

According to Professor Kessler, the distinction between the inquisitorial and accusatorial/adversarial models encompasses at least seven different aspects of the litigation:

(1) whether the court or the parties determine the litigation's scope and content,

(2) whether the court or the parties decide to initiate the litigation and to take the actions needed to move it forward,
(3) whether the litigation is composed of discrete stages, and whether steps not taken at a particular stage are thereafter precluded,
(4) whether the value of the proof is fixed formally, by rule or determined rationally, by free evaluation of the judge,
(5) whether proceedings are conducted in writing or orally and whether proof is written or oral,
(6) whether the court deals directly with the parties and witnesses, or indirectly through some intermediate agency, and
(7) whether proceedings are conducted in public, or in secret. Kessler, A. (2005). Our inquisitorial tradition: Equity procedure, due process, and the search for an alternative to the adversarial, 90 Cornell L. Review. 1181, 1223.

The key distinction is which entity controls the course of the case: the court, the government, the throne, one party, or the litigants?

Adversarial/Common Law Systems:

The adversarial system has its roots in the common law developed in Elizabethan England. Based on natural law at its inception, but swept by successive waves of positivism, the adversarial system is based upon two pillars: (1) that the judge, an impartial fact finder with broad discretion, sifts and winnows the truth from the competing presentations of the advocates (attorneys) of the contesting parties, and (2) the principle of *stare decisis,* that the same impartial judge then applies the text of the law to the controlling facts that he or she has found, in a fashion which harmonizes with the published decisions of past cases so as to create an uninterrupted interpretation of the law. Judges in the adversarial system have wide authority to interpret the law, but have little control over the initiation or scope of the litigation. Instead, the parties, but solely through designated professional functionaries (i.e., attorneys), interact with the judges to control the progress of the case. Upon the colonization of the New World, which became the United States of America, the adversarial system became the lode-star of the American legal system of jurisprudence. The former and current British Empire (Australia, Egypt, the Hong Kong Special Administrative District of the PRC, Ireland, India, Jordan, New Zealand, and Pakistan) and the British Isles are all adversarial/common law countries.

a. *Inquisitorial/ Civil Law Systems*

An illustrative example of the inquisitorial or civil law system is the Napoleonic Code; which was intended to reform the French legal system in accordance with the principles of the French Revolution: liberté, equalité, fraternité. The Napoleonic Code rejected the premise of natural law and is decidedly positivist. The Napoleonic Code, and its derivatives in other countries, is inquisitorial, in that the judge, not the parties, determines the initiation, scope, and extent of the litigation. Each case is unique before the court and will not usually serve as a precedent for other cases.

In civil law systems, the judge's ability to interpret the law is quite limited, the decisions are not published, and the common law concept of *stare decisis* does not operate. Consistency comes from the limitations placed upon the judge's ability to interpret the words of the statute, as opposed to simply applying the statute's words to the facts of the particular legal question at hand. Moreover, the legal professionals serve their clients only in an advisory role, with little direct interaction with the judges.

Following this analysis, *shari'a* may be seen as an exception, or substantial variation to the inquisitorial model. *Shari'a*, procedurally follows the inquisitorial model by using a fact finding judge with the power to define the scope of the investigation. The power of judges in a *shari'a* system, like that of the civil law, is limited to application, as opposed to interpretation. However, *shari'a* varies from the civil law model by being heavily influenced by a natural (moral) law theory. The distinctions between the rule of law systems are represented in Table 7-1.

Table 7-1
Comparison of Common Law and Civil Law. Shapiro, M.(1999). The Success of Judicial Review, in Kenney, Reisinger, and Reitz (eds.) Constitutional Dialogues in Comparative Perspective (New York: St. Martin's Press).

Common Law	**Civil Law**
Based on case law	Based on statutes
Emphasizes supra-statutory or natural legal rights	Positivism – statutes are sources of rights
Principal of *stare decisis* recognized, case-by-case inclusion and exclusion and analogy	Lawyer and judges work from statutory text
Adversarial	Inquisitorial

Non Rule-of-Law States
Religious/ Ruler/State-Made Law

The enforcement model for states where the law is both made and enforced by a supreme religious leader, a ruler or a state entity (such as a party) may have elements of the inquisitorial model. Here, an agent of the ruler/cleric/ party serving as the fact finder determines the scope of the inquiry and makes the final determination. However, the role of the agent and the limits of his or her decision making are strictly defined by the religious, ideological, or tribal source of the law. Interpretation of the law may be subject to influence or revision by the ruling/clerical/ party political element of the government.

In looking at the People's Republic of China, an evolving pattern may be noted. One writer noted that the Imperial China had long had "rule by law." However, the concept of shifting power from the central government to a truly independent judiciary would be a very broad step. (Peerenboom, 2000) Professor Peerenboom suggests that the explosive economic expansion in the PRC may shift power, but might only facilitate a system of rule of law because cross-cultural trade requires some predictability in enforcement (of laws). Further, as a first step, Peerenboom suggests that China first introduce *procedural* rule of law measures, such as an independent judiciary, rather than substantive measures such as a rule of *stare decisis*.

B. *Relative Advantages and Disadvantages of the Systems.*

Generally, the goal of any judicial system should be equal access to the adjudicator, as well as more predictable, factually linked, and rationally transparent results. (Miller and Pelato, 2004) The Adversarial/ Common Law systems should have all these attributes, because the parties largely control the initiation and pace of litigation, and the judicial officers are guided by the concepts of *stare decisis*. Moreover, the judges of the adversarial systems typically have wide discretion in interpreting the language of the laws.

However, the goals of a transactional quality of fact-based consistency and transparency in decisional logic are not always met by the adversarial model. Djankov et al, (2003), noted that English-model legal systems (Common Law) has significant cost due to incidence of litigation because of the ready ability of disputing parties to initiate and pursue lawsuits within the judicial systems as a means of seeking redress to legal disputes. Further, although to lesser degree than Civil law states, English model states had considerable "formalism," which led to less efficiency. Formalism is described as systems-embedded procedural requirements governing the initiation and prosecution of litigation, as well as requirements for legal professionals to pursue the litigation. Efficiency was reflected by the total time necessary to initiate, pursue, and conclude two sample legal actions, the eviction of non-paying tenant and the collection of a bad check.

Further, according to some critics of the American adversarial system, especially those advocating tort reforms, argue that the high cost of litigation, as well as the seeming unpredictability of outcomes of similar actions filed in differing states (e.g., Illinois or California auger for substantial limits on judicial discretion). Indeed, these parties argue that the lack of any cap or ceiling on monetary recovery for products liability and medical negligence liability claims make the system more like a game of chance than a system of justice. AMA (2005). Medical liability reform–now,http://www.ama-assn.org/go/mlrnow.

Alternately, the inquisitorial system or civil-code-based system has empirical support for perceived greater efficiency due to the Civil law's lesser emphasis on litigation. (Djankov et al, 2003). Thus, given the substantial limitation to the discretion of judges in civil law systems, coupled with the courts' control over the initiation of and continuation of litigation, data suggest that inquisitorial or civil law systems are slightly more efficient and substantially less costly. Moreover, civil law systems have a degree of predictability not seen in adversarial or common law systems, due to the limitation on discretion of the judges in interpreting the code.

On one level, the model most likely to meet this paradigm would be the religious, inquisitional model, because it is based upon a fixed source of law (natural law), which should manifestly give predictable results across variable, factual, transactional patterns for reasons that are readily apparent. However, one study suggests that at the lack of rigorous and uniform training for the clerics who are designated as the adjudicators has lead to quite differing results within the *shari'a* courts of at least one country, post 9/11 Afghanistan. (Miller, L. and Perito, R. (2004). Establishing the Rule of law in Afghanistan. U.S. Institute of Peace Special Report No. 117, U. S Institute of Peace, p.5).

***

What are the Change Agents for the Organization within the Legal Domain?

There are many scholars who have summarized the work of change theorists. One is C. M. Christiansen, who postulated a three-stage method for defining a detailed strategy to guide a company.

He describes the three stages as 1) identifying the driving forces, 2) formulating a strategy to address those driving forces, and 3) creating a plan to implement that strategy. Change agents within the legal domain are those entities that have the power to influence changes in the interpretation or formulation of the law. Change agents will differ according to the distinctions between rule of law and non rule of law legal systems.

1.   *Rule of Law Countries*

A.   *Adversarial/Common Law*

Within the Adversarial system, the entities that have the ability to change the interpretation or formulation of the law include the members of the judiciary, the legal professionals who advocate specific interpretations to the judges during litigation, as well as the legislatures that promulgate new laws or changes to existing laws. Moreover, in countries such as the United States, which have a federal system of state governments, judges and legislators in each of the several states serve as potential change agents. Finally, given the ready access to legislative representatives in most Common Law countries, lobbyists, paid or unpaid, may also be viewed as change agents. A note of caution here, for in the United States, a concerted effort by one political party to consolidate its lobbying within the "K Street Project" has had negative effects for that party. See Scahill, J.(2006, February). Exile on k street. The Nation. http://www. The nation. Retrieved June 3006. Nonetheless, from the organization's point of view, the plethora of potential change agents within this system put a premium on the organization's ability to freely interact and communicate with the change agents.

B.   *Inquisitorial/ Civil Law*

Conversely, the same factors that facilitate substantial potential for change within the Adversarial system impair the effectiveness of a plethora of change agents within the Inquisitorial, Civil Law system. Here, both judges and legal professionals are significantly limited in their ability to effect change through broadened interpretations of the law. Organizations seeking change must resort to the members of the legislature to effect changes in laws affecting the organization. Moreover, because many Civil Law countries tend to have stronger central governments and weaker state or provincial governments, the focus on change agents will be on the central government. From the organization's viewpoint, the establishment and continuation of relationships with members of the central government is a key element for effecting change.

2. *Non Rule of Law States*

Within these countries, effecting change is both simpler and more complicated. As the legal systems of these countries place institutional reliance on the continuing validity of the underlying religion or ideology, change is disfavored. Effecting modifications to interpretations of the law or significant changes to the law requires a delicate distinction between re-interpretation, on the one hand, and religious or political heresy on the other. That said, economic development has been suggested as a mechanism for change in countries that heretofore have not had and established rule of law. It has been said that the burgeoning economic change in the People's Republic of China cannot help but bring about the advance of the Rule of Law in that country. One group of scholars, (Djankov et al, 2003) however, suggests that the jury may still be out on that question. Another commentator, Blodgett, H. (2005), a former financial and securities analyst writing in Slate, The OnLine Magazine, suggests that the Chinese leadership may be seeking a form of capitalism without such democratic notions as the Rule of Law.

C. *Organizational Operations in the Legal Domain*

Given this global analysis, what conclusions may organizational leaders draw for optimizing their operations? First and foremost, as noted above, the opportunity to facilitate change within the legal domain is radically different between the domain of Rule of Law nations (those with independent judiciaries) and Non Rule of Law nations. Moreover, the location and efficiency of those change agents is significantly different within nations following either of the two Rule of Law systems. Second, the legal domains within Natural Law based systems with Adversarial enforcement will differ from Legal Positivist Systems with Inquisitorial enforcement. Finally, operation within Rule of law nations will differ markedly from those in Non Rule of Law nations.

Operations in Rule of Law nations will be markedly more predictable and reliable, whether in an Adversarial or Inquisitorial system. The operations will also be occasioned by the cost and risk restraints of litigation and formalism, as discussed above. In Inquisitorial or Civil Law countries, more linear predictions may be made for operations based on the limitations on those nations' judges to apply the law rather interpret it. That said, Civil Law nations do carry the burden of greater government regulation and the accompanying temporal and financial cost. As with the decentralized judiciary seen in the United States, an Adversarial or Common Law nation brings its unique challenges to the organization. For example, due to the influence of regional customs, judges may interpret laws in differing manners. Witness the regional differences in the decisions testing the validity of "Blue Laws," a product of the American Puritan era, which prohibited the operations of most businesses on the Sabbath. (Christian Science Monitor, 2003, December 050. http://www.csmonitor.com/ 2003/1205/p01s02). Where Blue Laws were once the standard until the end of the Second World War, fewer than five states, including Utah, still limit business and alcohol sales on Sunday.

Operations in Non Rule of Law nations will be at once simpler and more complicated, especially in nations with a theocratic legal system. Given this legal domain's significant reliance on religious text, and the belief in the inerrant nature of that text, an organization's operations will be constrained to the extent that day to day operations include activities inconsistent with the theocratic law. For example, consider the Kingdom of Saudi Arabia, considered here as a Non Rule of Law country due to the lack of an independent judiciary. (US Department of State, 2005. Country Report p. 2.). Western business women doing business in the Kingdom are impaired as business agents because women are treated as a lesser class under that country's law. (US Department of State, 2005. Country Report p. 4). Likewise, when operating outside your home legal domain, such as the Western business women, for good or ill, a thorough working knowledge of the underlying theory supporting the law of a country is essential for effective business.

This is not to say that an organization's operations will always be severely constrained in Non Rule of Law nations. Witness the Peoples Republic of China, an avowedly communist, Marxist-Leninist state. The explosive commercial intercourse between the Middle Kingdom and the West in the last 10 years has brought about change in day to day business operations in the PRC. That the leadership of the Communist Party of China can embrace capitalism, the anathema of Karl Marx' *Das Kapital*, manifests the potential for significant change in the source for that nation's law, the party ideology. The lesson for organizational leaders is that all legal domains are found along the continuum between the fixed site of morals and the transitory site of ethics.

***

Part III Summary

We have reviewed the significance of the legal domain of the SPELIT POWER MATRIX to the organization. That question is first approached by distinguishing between morality, universal statements of right and wrong; ethics, a society's ongoing determination of acceptable and not acceptable behavior; and law, the codification of duties owed by persons within a society to one another. Natural Law and Legal Positivism are studied as foundations for the differing architectures of systems for enforcing law in Rule of Law systems which have evolved as the Adversarial/ Common Law system and the Inquisitorial/ Civil Law system. The efficacy of the operation of a legal system in the absence of an independent judicial system is address in the discussion of Non Rule of Law countries. Change agents are identified by analyzing distinctions in enforcement regimes within the differing legal systems. Finally, the chapter analyzes the distinctions of operating within differing legal and enforcement regimes.

The next chapter will discuss the intercultural environment of SPELIT.

***

References and Suggested Readings

Ethics and Law, generally

Christiansen, C. M., (1997) Making strategy: Learning by doing. Harvard Business Review, 3 (12).

Horner, J. (2004). Morality, ethics, and law: Introductory concepts. Seminars in Speech and Language 24, pp. 263-274.

Schmieder-Ramirez, J. and Mallette, L., (2005). An Introduction to the SPELIT© interdisciplinary analysis methodology, Abstract Rev 3-15, Pepperdine University, Graduate School of Education and Psychology, 2005.

Tansey Martens, L. (2003). Transatlantic perspectives on business ethics training. International Business Ethics Review, 6 (1). http://www.business-ethics.org/newsdetail .asp?newsid=44. Retrieved, June 2006.

Christian Science Monitor, (2003, December 05). In the battle for Sunday, the 'blue laws' are falling. The Christian ScienceMonitor.http://www.csmonitor.com/2003/1205/p01s02, Retrieved June, 2006.

Natural Law

Aquinas, Thomas, On Law, Morality and Politics, (Indianapolis, Hackett Publishing Co. 1988)

Marmor, A. (2001) The nature of law. The Stanford Encyclopedia of Philosophy, Edward N. Zalta (ed.). http://plato.stanford.edu/archives/sum2001/entries/lawphil-nature/>. Retrieved, May 2006.

Legal Positivism

Bentham, Jeremy (1782). Of Laws in General, Ed. H.L.A. Hart, (London, Athelon/Athlone Press 1970).

Hart, H.L.A. (1958). Positivism and the separation of law and morals. 71 Harvard Law Review, 593, repr. In Essays in Jurisprudence and Philosophy (Oxford, Clarendon Press, 1983).

Himma, K E. (1999). Positivism, naturalism, and the obligation to obey the law. Abstract, Southern Journal of Philosophy, 36 (2).

Comparative Law

American Medical Association (2005). Medical liability reform–now. October 19, 2005. http://www.ama-assn.org/go/mlrnow. (Retrieved, June 2006)

Blodget, H., (2005). China's biggest gamble; Can it have capitalism without democracy? A prediction. Slate, The Online Magazine. http://www.slate.com/id/2117169/ Retrieved, June 2006.

Djankov, S., La Porta, R., Lopez-de-Silanes, F., Shleifer, A., (2003). Courts. Quarterly Journal of Economics 118 (2), pp. 453-517.

Kessler, A., (2005). Our inquisitorial tradition: Equity, procedure, due process, and the search for an alternative to the adversarial. 90 Cornell L. Rev. 1181.

Mattei, U., Antoniolli, L. and Rossato, A., (2000). Comparative law and economics, in Bouckaert, Boudewijn and De Geest, Gerrit (eds.), Encyclopedia of Law and Economics, Volume I. The History and Methodology of Law and Economics, (Cheltenham, Edward Elgar Press, 2000).

Miller, L. and Perito, R., (2004). Establishing the rule of law in Afghanistan. U.S. Institute of Peace Special Report No. 117, U. S Institute of Peace. http://www.usip.org/pubs/specialreports/sr117.html. Retrieved, May 2006.

Peerenboom, R., (2000). China and the rule of law: Part I. Perspectives 1 (5), Overseas Young Chinese Forum. 2000. Retrieved, May 2006 from: http://www.oycf.org/Perspectives /5_043000/china_and_the_rule_of_law.htm. (Note: This, the first of a two-part essay, excerpts and summarizes some of the main points from two longer articles, "Ruling the Country in Accordance with Law: Reflections on the Rule and Role of Law in Contemporary China," Cultural Dynamics 11:3 (1999): 315-351, and a revised and expanded version of that article, which is forthcoming in Chinese in Zhongguo shehui zhuanxing shiqi de falu fazhan— zhongmei xuezhe lunwenji (Falu Chubanshe, 2000). These two articles, which contain full citations and footnotes, are available by emailing: peerenbo@law.ucla.ed

Scahill, J (2006, February 20). Exile on k street. The Nation. http://www.thenation.com/doc/20060220/scahill. Retrieved, June 2006.

United States Department of State, (2005). Country report for the kingdom of Saudi Arabia. http://www.state.gov/g/drl/rls/hrrpt/2004/41731.htm. Retrieved June 2006

Chapter 8
Analyzing the Intercultural Dynamics Within an Organization

Gale R. Mazur
Michael A. Moodian

***

Introduction

In *The Art of Worldly Wisdom*, Baltasar Gracian (1647/1993) states "Live with those from whom you can learn; let friendly intercourse be a school for knowledge, and social contact, a school for culture" (p. 6). All organizations have intercultural dynamics in which members must deal with issues of acceptance and adaptation to differences in dealing with employees, suppliers, and customers. When organizations value and encourage the acceptance and integration of different ideas and practices, they maximize the benefits of a diverse workforce and marketplace. To provide a framework for analyzing the intercultural environment of an organization, this chapter will focus on strategies to analyze and assess the multicultural competence of an organization.

***

Background and Definition of Terms

Before providing an analytical framework for assessing the intercultural environment of an organization, the meanings of culture, intercultural sensitivity, intercultural competence, and cultural intelligence must be established. Culture is a system of shared meanings comprised of the actions, values, and beliefs that develop within an organization and guide the behavior of its members (Morgan, 2000; Robbins, 2005). Through culture, individuals learn how to perceive the world, interpret stimuli, and respond to stimuli (Parillo, 2000). Intercultural sensitivity describes how individuals comprehend culturally based differences (Bhawuk & Brislin, 1992), while intercultural competence explains the extent to which people can navigate through their differences (J. Bennett & M. Bennett, 2003). Cultural intelligence refers to the degree that you are able to cognitively, physically, and emotionally adapt to a secondary culture (Earley and Mosakowski, 2004).

Prior to conducting an intercultural environment assessment, it is necessary to review the field of cross-cultural studies from a historical perspective. If society is the structure of human behavior, then culture is the glue, or underlying factors that hold society together. Anthropologist Edward T. Hall is credited with beginning the study of intercultural communications with the publication of his book, *The Silent Language*, in 1959, which discussed non-verbal communication and the concepts of space and time in the transmission of messages. Written for the general public, Hall's book became a best seller that aroused scholarly interest in studying intercultural communication. Differences in verbal and non-verbal and direct and indirect communication styles were studied and the impact on intercultural relationships identified. (Rogers, Hart & Miike, 2002; Bennett, 1998).

As research into communications styles expanded, differences in values among cultures were identified by Hofstede (1980, 1991). By examining data on the values of 100,000 IBM employees located in over 53 different cultures and countries, Hofstede argued that cultural differences are significant among countries. He identified four critical values including power distance, individualism verses collectivism, masculinity verses femininity, and uncertainty avoidance. In making brief national generalizations, Hofstede found that individualistic countries such as Australia and the United States encourage independence, whereas collective societies such as Taiwan and Pakistan take responsibility for others' welfare. Cultures of low power distance such as Great Britain and Sweden respect leaders but may challenge their decisions; high power cultures such as Malaysia and Mexico are more likely to accept the decisions made by the leader in power. Cultures with masculine orientations such as Japan and Venezuela value the acquisition of money and tangible possessions over caring for people and quality of life; feminine cultures such as Chile and Norway are more concerned about relationships and the quality of life. Countries with high uncertainty avoidance such as Greece and Venezuela prefer stability and security; cultures comfortable with unstructured situations frequently caused by rapid change include India and Hong Kong. Although individuals within a culture may hold different values, Hofstede concluded that different countries had different cultural identities (Hofstede, 1980, 1991).

Recognizing different communication styles and values among cultures, Milton Bennett advanced the work by exploring how people adapt to other cultures. Bennett (2004) created the Developmental Model of Intercultural Sensitivity, which measures intercultural competence in adapting behavior appropriately in different cultural environments. As students were observed in intercultural workshops, classes, graduate and international exchange programs, it became evident that they handled cultural differences in predictable ways. As their experience of cultural differences became more sophisticated, their intercultural competence increased. From these observations, six stages of intercultural competence were developed and validated; the ethnocentric stages include Denial, Defense and Minimization, and what he coins the *ethnorelative* stages of Acceptance, Adaptation, and Integration (Bennett & Bennett, 2004). *Enthnorelativism* is a term that refers to advanced levels of intercultural competence, specifically, a representation of the idea that you can place your socially constructed reality in context with multiple other realities. One who displays ethnorelativity has a tendency to successfully adapt into different cultures.

Earley and Mosakowski (2004) furthered the concept of ethnorelativity by introducing Cultural Intelligence (CQ) as the ability to effectively alter your behavior according to the surrounding culture that you are in. One who displays the highest level of CQ is able to understand the underlying dynamics within various groups, thus adapting into various actions and behaviors to eventually achieve successful integration. The CQ diagnosis model is comprised of cognitive, physical, and emotional components. Cognitive CQ refers to the inquisitive process that you experience internally when determining a strategy for attempting to approach cultural difference. Physical CQ refers to the degree that you are able to alter speech, body language, and expressions when integrating into a new culture. Lastly, emotional/motivational CQ relates to the degree of confidence that your have in adapting to cultural difference (Earley and Mosakowski, 2004).

***

SPELIT and the Intercultural Environment

The intercultural environment has significant relationships to the social, political, economic, legal, and technological environments.

Although the focus of this chapter is the intercultural, a brief discussion of its connection and impact on the other environments follows.

Intercultural competence impacts the social environment, particularly because cultures exist based on ethnic background, gender, generations, sexual orientation, and various other factors. Studies show that productivity within organizations increases when individuals within the organization have the ability to work together effectively and embrace diversity (Hampden-Turner & Trompenaars, 1997). While more conflict may exist in heterogeneous teams versus homogeneous groups, heterogeneous teams typically outperform groups that are less diverse, thus leading to further profitability for organizations (Robbins, 2005).

In reference to the political environment, in government, the decision-making and issues of power are highly influenced by issues of intercultural competence. In a system that is socially stratified by economic class, it can be argued that the power elite utilize status and social networks to maintain their hold of power (Higley, 2000, Mills, 1956/2000). Such a stratification system that is based on economic class often corresponds with a social hierarchy among ethnic minorities in the U.S. A leader who demonstrates a high level of intercultural competence can be adequately prepared to deal more effectively with pertinent issues across all social classes. Additionally, political leaders who cannot demonstrate intercultural sensitivity will not be effective in leading diverse groups or building international relationships. (Earley and Mosakowski, 2004, Tzu, 1910/2003).

In relating to the economic environment, trends of globalization are requiring American companies to conduct business internationally. In carrying out international operations, the need for higher levels of intercultural competence are required to ensure a more cohesive working environment, which would ultimately lead to greater bottom-line results (Bhagwati, 2004). The focus of diversity training to address such issues resolves around valuing individual differences, abolishing stereotypes, and increasing multicultural awareness (Robbins, 2005).

From a legal perspective in the United States, it is in the best interest of organizations to maintain a diverse workforce that practices inclusion to adhere to the spirit as well as the letter of Equal Opportunity. Oftentimes, members of organizations are required to attend cross-cultural competence training sessions to meet compliance regulations and protect the legal interests of the organization (J.M. Bennett & M.J. Bennett, 2004).

Finally, the technology environment has played a dramatic role in the youth in the United States. Through the Information Age and the explosion of mass commercialization, cultural patterns have been created that have led to individuals seeking instant gratification.

Attention spans have shortened and commercial products have been tailored toward quickness and further efficiency, correlating with a new youth culture (Generation Y) that is revolutionizing the intergroup dynamics of modern organizations (Croteau & Hoynes, 2000).

***

Intercultural Environment Assessment

In contemporary America, many organizations are facing a multicultural workforce that is diverse along racial, ethnic, gender, religious, and sexual identity lines (Winslow, Kummhuber & Soeters, 2004). To assist with optimum organizational effectiveness, there is an increased importance in nurturing intercultural competence within organizations to deal with such cultural differences. Bicultural and multiculturally competent individuals and organizations are able to adapt their behavior to function effectively within one or more different cultures. This requires accepting alternative ways of thinking and behaving even when there is disagreement with a belief or action. Individuals and organizations that possess intercultural competence are able to function comfortably and successfully when confronted with cultures, values, and practices very different from their own (Adler, 1977; Bennett, 2004).

Intercultural competence does not come easily or naturally. Enculturation starts very early when children are taught how to behave and think by family, friends, and educators; this socialization process is reinforced by organizations that promise continued employment, promotion, and other rewards for adhering to cultural norms. Individuals develop cultural identity by learning to interpret and understand verbal and nonverbal messages sent by those with whom they live and work (Kim, 2004). Religious teachings offer an example of the impact of enculturation. Most major religions, including Hinduism, Islam, and Buddhism, encourage followers to practice what Christianity calls the *golden rule,* which is to treat others as you would want to be treated. Rather than recognize differences in values, beliefs, and behaviors, the golden rule assumes similarity across peoples and cultures. While this has been a prevailing ideology across egalitarian cultures for hundreds of years, the limitations of the golden rule are that it implies that a differing culture is either as complex or as simple as your own. Thus we may neglect to focus on cultural difference beyond a superficial level. Interculturalists and organizations suggest that the golden rule needs to be replaced with what has been called the platinum rule, which is treating others as others want to be treated (Bennett, 1966).

Enculturation occurs in every environment. And although it is natural, it can lead to ethnocentrism, which is defined as using your own beliefs, values, and customs to judge all cultures consciously or unconsciously (Bennett, 1966). For example, most Americans would not eat horse or dog meat but regularly consume beef and chicken. If ethnocentric, they discount and disapprove of cultures that eat meats they do not eat, and at the same time they may discount and disapprove of cultures that object to killing animals for food. When one is ethnocentric, she or he may consider other cultures as deviants from the norm (i.e., they equate the norm with their own cultural worldview). Becoming ethnorelative entails being comfortable and adapting to different beliefs, value, and customs in different cultures and requires a transition of moving through several distinct stages. (Bennett, 2004; Thomas & Inkson, 2005).

Determining intercultural competence requires a combination of cognitive, emotional, and behavioral assessments (Bennett & Bennett, 2004, Earley 2004; Thomas, 2005). Cognitive development evaluates how much knowledge and understanding you have of the impact of culture on attitudes and behavior. Emotional growth occurs as your willingness and confidence in handling cross-cultural situations increases. Behaviorally, intercultural competence is measured in the individual's ability to develop effective strategies and act appropriately in different cultural situations.

***

Intercultural Competence Models

There are a variety of models and instruments that have been developed to describe and measure cultural intelligence and intercultural competence (Exhibit X). The Development Model of Intercultural Sensitivity (DMIS) created by M.J. Bennett (1986, 1993, 1998, 2004) has been selected as a framework for discussing intercultural competence because it is backed by extensive research and validation and offers a clear and measurable progression from ethnocentrism to ethnorelativism for both individuals and organizations. The following discussion will define the different developmental stages of intercultural competence for individuals and organizations, describing cognitive, affective, and behavioral assessments at each stage.

As illustrated in Figure 8-1, the Development Model of Intercultural Sensitivity (DMIS) created by M. J. Bennett (1986, 1993, 1998, 2004) includes six stages, with the first three classified as ethnocentric. Individuals in these first stages view all cultures through the lens of their own beliefs, values, and customs. As individuals and organizations progress, they become more ethnorelative and increasingly comfortable adapting to different cultures with different beliefs, values, and customs. A brief description of each stage in the DMIS model follows.

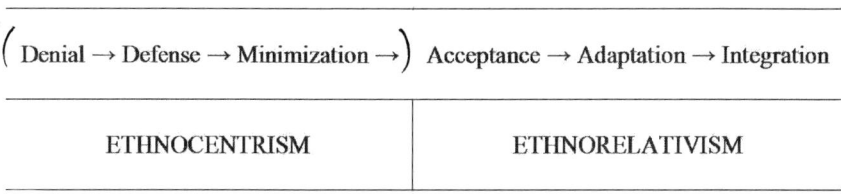

Figure 8-1. The Development Model of Intercultural Sensitivity (DMIS)

Denial

In the DMIS model, the first developmental stage is denial, which is characterized by indifference or ignorance of cultural differences. Individuals in denial have little knowledge of other cultures, no interest in learning about them, and prefer homogeneity. Oftentimes, those who practice denial exert a polarized worldview and are the products of a monocultural socialization process. Organizations in denial are insular, disregard cultural differences, and may be criticized for being disrespectful of cultural differences. They likely exert no commitment or systemic effort to recruit and retain a diverse workforce (Bennett, 1986, 1993, 1998, 2004)

Defense

The second developmental stage of the DMIS model is defense. Recognizing that cultural differences exist, those in defense are characterized by polarization and "we-they" thinking. Believing their culture is superior, they denigrate other cultures as backward and underdeveloped. Segregation is encouraged by dominant groups who want to protect their status and privilege, as well as by minorities who want promote ethnic heritage and uniqueness. Organizations in the defense stage view cultural differences as an obstacle to overcome; diversity programs may be instituted but often fail. The attitude of superiority and "knowing best" is often interpreted as arrogance, and combativeness may occur in managing international relationships. It is possible that someone may do a reversal in defense by seeing another culture as superior while maligning their own (Bennett, 1986, 1993, 1998, 2004). This description is not unlike a profile of cultural intelligence (CQ) that Earley offers; he describes someone as provincial (2004, p. 142) if they are effective only when working with others who have similar backgrounds and values.

Minimization

In the DMIS model, the final stage of ethnocentrism is minimization, in which individuals recognize but ignore cultural differences by focusing on similarities, and assuming that all people are fundamentally the same and want the same things. Individuals in minimization accept superficial cultural differences such as food and dress but mistake their values as universal desires. Attempts to behave appropriately cross-culturally are often based on "being nice" in your own cultural terms. As an example, Americans engaging in minimization may believe that people everywhere want freedom, democracy, and a competitive marketplace. Organizations in minimization overestimate their cultural sensitivity, and may not understand why recruitment efforts for diversity programs are successful but retention is poor. By emphasizing universal values and principles, cultural conformity is imposed (Bennett, 1986, 1993, 1998, 2004).

Acceptance

As individuals transition from minimization into acceptance, they evolve from being ethnocentric to ethnorelative. Recognizing that each culture has a unique and intertwined system of values, beliefs, attitudes, and norms that give meaning, significance, and cultural identity, they understand that one culture is not measurably better or more civilized than another (Adler, 1977). In acceptance, individuals recognize distinct cultural contexts that provide frameworks to analyze differences among cultures. They are curious, non-evaluative about cultural difference, and actively seek information and experiences to build intercultural competence. Organizations acknowledge cultural differences but are often unclear about how to address them, which may lead to "talking the talk" but not "walking the walk" (Bennett, 1986, 1993, 1998, 2004). They could be described as analysts who systemically employ a variety of strategies to identify and understand cultural rules and norms, and "mimics" who respond appropriately to cultural clues but may not understand their significance (Earley, 2004, pp. 143—5).

Adaptation

Individuals at this stage of development are able to use their knowledge about their own and other cultures to intentionally shift their cultural frame of reference and put themselves in "the other person's shoes." Aware of other cultural perspectives, these individuals are empathic and able to modify their behavior appropriately in different cultures. Many seem to be naturals who are able to rely on intuition and usually are right (Earley, 2004, p. 143). Organizations at this level value intercultural competence as an essential leadership skill and encourage ongoing employee training and skill development (Bennett, 1986, 1993, 1998, 2004). With a strong commitment and respect for diversity, organizations are committed to business strategies that benefit from intercultural teams (Janssens & Brett, 2006).

Integration

Persons at the final stage of the DMIS model are classified under the ideal state of ethnorelativity and complete intercultural competence. Able to interpret and evaluate behavior from a variety of cultural frames, they believe there is never a single right way or just one right answer. Describing an individual who can transparently move into another culture as a chameleon, Earley (2004) found that only 5% of the managers that he studied had this capability. In multiculturally competent organizations, there is little emphasis on ethnic or national identity. Issues, policies, and actions are evaluated in the appropriate cultural context. Ethics and morality are not seen as absolute and universal but are viewed from different perspectives and as different realities (Bennett, 1986, 1993, 1998, 2004; Triandis, 2006).

Intercultural competence can be developed but requires strong commitment to gain knowledge and understanding of other cultures as well as the motivation and desire to behave differently (Brislin, Worthley & MacNab, 2006; Ng & Earley, 2006). Extensive research involving over 2000 managers in 60 countries (Earley & Mosakowski, 2004), university-level study abroad programs (Cushner & Karim, 2004), Peace Corps volunteers (Bennhold-Samaan, 2004), and the armed forces (Winslow, Kammhuber & Soeters, 2004) have demonstrated that intercultural competence can be learned and developmental progress measured.

The development of intercultural competence frequently and effectively begins with an assessment of the competencies and needs of the individual and/or organization (Landis, Bennett & Bennett, 2004). Table 8-1 highlights a variety of assessment instruments, including the

Intercultural Development Inventory, which was developed by Bennett based on the DMIS described above.

Table 8-1
Intercultural Assessment Instruments

Instrument	Source
Assessing Diversity Climate	Kossek & Zonia, 1993
Intercultural Development Inventory	Hammer, Bennett, & Wiseman, 2003
Intercultural Sensitivity Inventory	Bhawuk & Brislin, 1992
Intercultural Conflict Style Inventory	Hammer, 2005

Each of these instruments measure different components of intercultural sensitivity. For example, Hammer (2005) offers the Intercultural Conflict Style scales, which categorize four primary conflict styles that correlate with cultural socialization processes. The four styles identified are *discussion* (disagreement by direct confrontation with emotional restraint, prevalent in Northern European and American cultures), *engagement* (disagreement by direct confrontation with emotional expressiveness, prevalent in African American, Russian, and Greek cultures), *accommodation* (disagreement by indirection confrontation with emotional restraint, prevalent in Japanese and Southeast Asian cultures) and *dynamic* (disagreement by indirection with emotional expressiveness, prevalent in Arab cultures). Understanding the different conflict styles enables individuals and organizations to approach and manage it successfully in a variety of cultural environments.

***

Summary

Understanding, valuing, and accepting difference is critical to the success of individuals and organizations in today's global economy, and the development of intercultural competence maximizes the potential benefits of a diverse workforce and marketplace. This chapter has provided a framework for analyzing and evaluating the intercultural environment of organizations by suggesting that achieving intercultural competence requires the progression through six unique stages, and the development at each stage includes cognitive, affective, and behavioral components. Moving from ethnocentrism to ethnorelativism is essential to prosper and perhaps even survive in today's global economy.

The next chapter will discuss the technology environment of SPELIT.

***

References

Adler, P.S. (1977). Beyond cultural identity: Reflections on multiculturalism. In Bennett, M.J. (ed.). *Basic concepts of intercultural communication.* (p. 225—246). Yarmouth, ME: Intercultural Press.

Bennett, J.M., & Bennett, M.J. (2004). Developing intercultural sensitivity: An integrative approach to global and domestic diversity. In D. Landis, J. M. Bennett, & M. J. Bennett (Eds.), *Handbook of intercultural training.* (3rd ed., pp. 147–165). Thousand Oaks, CA: Sage.

Bennett, M.J. (1986). A developmental approach to training for intercultural sensitivity.
International Journal of Intercultural Relations (1), 179-196.

Bennett, M. (2004). Becoming interculturally competent. In J. Wurzel (Ed.), *Toward multiculturalism: A reader in multicultural education* (2nd ed., pp. 62–77). Newton, MA: Intercultural Resource Corporation.

Bennett, M.J. (2004). Intercultural communication: A current perspective. In Bennett, M.J. (ed.). *Basic concepts of intercultural communication.* (p. 1—34). Yarmouth, ME: Intercultural Press.

Bennett, M.J. (1966). Overcoming the golden rule: Sympathy and empathy. In Bennett, M.J. (ed.). *Basic concepts of intercultural communication.* (p. 337—362). Yarmouth, ME: Intercultural Press.

Bennett, M.J. (1993). Toward ethnorelativism: A developmental model of intercultural sensitivity. In Paige, R.M. (ed.). *Education for the intercultural experience.* (2nd ed., p. 21—71). Yarmouth, ME: Intercultural Press.

Bennhold-Samaan, L. (2004). The evolution of cross-cultural training in the Peace Corps. In Landis, D., Bennett, J.M., & Bennett, M.J. (eds.). *Handbook of intercultural training.* (p. 363—394). Thousand Oaks, CA: Sage.

Bhagwati, J. (2004). *In defense of globalization.* New York: Oxford University Press.

Bhawuk, D.P.S., & Brislin, R. (1992). The measurement of intercultural sensitivity using the concepts of individualism and collectivism. *International Journal of Intercultural Relations,* 16, 413-436.

Brislin, R., Worthley, R., & Macnab, B. (2006, Feb). Cultural intelligence: Understanding behaviors that serve people's goals". *Group and Organizational Management, 31*(1), 40.

Croteau, D., & Haynes, W. (2000). *Media Society: Industries, images, and audiences.* Thousand Oaks, CA: Pine Forge Press.

Cushner, K. & Karim, A.U. (2004). Study abroad at the university level. In Landis, D., Bennett, J.M., & Bennett, M.J. (eds.). *Handbook of intercultural training.* (p. 289—308). Thousand Oaks, CA: Sage.

Earley, P., & Mosakowski, E. (2004, October). Cultural intelligence. *Harvard Business Review, 82*(10), 139–146.

Gracian, B. (1647/1993). *The art of worldly wisdom* (M. Fischer, trans.). New York: Barnes & Noble Books.

Hammer, M.R. (2005). The intercultural conflict style inventory: A conceptual framework and measure of intercultural conflict resolution approaches. *International Journal of Intercultural Relations, 29*(6), 675-695.

Hammer, M.R., Bennett, M.J., & Wiseman, R. (2003). Measuring intercultural sensitivity: The intercultural development inventory. *International Journal of Intercultural Relations, 27*(4), 421-443.

Hampden-Turner, C., & Trompenaars, F. (1997). *Riding the waves of culture: Understanding diversity in global business.* New York: McGraw-Hill.

Higley, S.R. (2000). Privilege, power and place: The geography of the American upper class. In T. E. Ore (Ed.), *The social construction of difference and inequality: Race, class, gender and sexuality* (pp. 91–105). Mountain View, CA: Mayfield Publishing Company.

Hofstede, G. (1980). *Culture's consequences: International differences in work-related values.* Beverly Hills, CA: Sage Publications.

Hofstede, G. (1991). *Cultures and organizations: Software of the mind.* New York: McGraw-Hill.

Janssens, M. & Brett, J.M.. (2006, Feb.). Cultural intelligence in global teams: A fusion model of collaboration. *Group and Organizational Management, 31*(1), 64.

Kim, Y.Y. (2004). Long-term cross-cultural adaptation: Training implications of an integrative theory. In Landis, D., Bennett, J.M., & Bennett, M.J. (eds.). *Handbook of intercultural training.* (p. 337—362). Thousand Oaks, CA: Sage.

Kossek, E.E., & Zonia, S.C. (1993). Assessing diversity climate: A field study of reactions to employer efforts to promote diversity. *Journal of Organizational Behavior,* 14, 61-81.

Landis, D; Bennett; J. M. & Bennett; M. J., *Handbook of intercultural training.* (3rd ed., pp. 1—10). Thousand Oaks, CA: Sage.

Mills, C.W. (1956/2000). *The power elite.* Oxford: Oxford University Press.

Morgan, G. (1998). *Images of organization* (2nd ed.). Thousand Oaks, CA: Sage Publications.

Ng, K., & Earley, P. C. (2006, Feb.). Culture + intelligence: Old constructs, new frontiers. *Group and Organizational Management, 31*(1).

Reiman, J. (2001). *The rich get richer and the poor get prison: Ideology, class, and criminal justice* (6th ed.). Needham Heights, MA: Allyn and Bacon.

Robbins, S.P. (2005). *Essentials of organizational behavior* (8th ed.). Upper Saddle River, NJ: Pearson Prentice Hall.

Rogers, E.M., Hart, W.B. & Miike, Y.. (2002). Edward T. Hall and the history of intercultural communication: The United States and Japan. *Keio Communication Review. 24.*

Thomas, D. C., (2006, Feb.). Domain and development of cultural intelligence: The importance of mindfulness. *Group and Organizational Management, 31*(1).

Thomas, D. C., & Inkson, K. (2005). Cultural intelligence: People skills for a global workplace. *Consulting to Management, 16*(1), 5—9.

Triandis, H.C. (2006, Feb.). Cultural intelligence in organizations.. *Group and Organizational Management, 31*(1).

Tzu, S. (1910/2003). *The art of war* (L. Giles, trans.) New York: Barnes & Noble Books.

Winslow, D., Kammhuber, S. Soeters, J.L.. (2004). Diversity management and training in non-American forces. In Landis, D., Bennett, J.M., & Bennett, M.J. (eds.). *Handbook of intercultural training.* (p. 289—308). Thousand Oaks, CA: Sage.

***

Recommendations for Further Reading

Bennett, M. (ed.). (1998). *Basic concepts of intercultural communication.* Yarmouth, ME: Intercultural Press.

Carr-Ruffino, N. (1996). *Managing diversity: People skills for a multicultural workplace.* Albany, NY: International Thomson.

Condon, J., & Yousef, F. (1985). *An introduction to intercultural communication.* New York: Macmillan.

Earley, P., Ang, S., & Tan, J. (2005). *CQ: Developing cultural intelligence at work.* Stanford University Press.

González, A., Houston, M., & Chen, V. (1997). *Our voices: Essays in culture, ethnicity, and communication: An intercultural anthology* (2nd ed). Los Angeles: Roxbury.

Gudykunst, W. B., Ting-Toomey, S., & Chua, E. (1988). *Culture and interpersonal communication. vol. 8: Interpersonal communication series.* Newbury Park, CA: Sage.

Hofstede, G. (1991). *Cultures and organizations: Software of the mind.* London: McGraw-Hill.

Kohls, L. R. (1996). *Survival kit for overseas living* (3rd ed.). Yarmouth, ME: Intercultural Press.

Lustig, M., & Koester, J. (1999). *Intercultural competence: Interpersonal communication across cultures.* New York: Longman.

Martin, J.N., & Nakayama, T.K. (1997). *Intercultural communication in contexts.* Mountain View, CA: Mayfield.

Paige, R. M., (ed.). (1993). *Education for the intercultural experience.* Yarmouth, ME: Intercultural Press, 1993.

Ponterotto, J., & Pedersen, P. (1993). *Preventing prejudice: A guide for counselors and educators.* Newbury Park, CA: Sage.

Stewart, E. C., & Bennett, M.J. (1991). *American cultural patterns: A cross-cultural perspective.* Yarmouth, ME: Intercultural Press.

Thomas, D. C., & Inkson, K. (2004). *Cultural intelligence: People skills for a global workplace.* Berrett-Koehler Publishers

Chapter 9
The Technology Component of the SPELIT Environmental Analysis Model

Dr. Maurice Shihadi Ed.D.
Adjuncts.net and Anacru.com

***

Introduction

Technology assessment is the last component of the SPELIT environmental analysis model. It is used as a cyclical process to not only align, but strategically focus efforts of higher level managers to use technology for increased levels of profit, marketing, and service quality. As such, it must be clearly focused on how employees relate to the technology in use as opposed to the cost, efficiency, or usefulness of the technology itself. In order to retain this focus, the facilitator of the technology assessment needs to be able to (a) communicate about technology using non-technical language; (b) understand the overall corporate strategy and goals; (c) have the support of management to collaborate with other departments; (d) possess a skill set conducive to customer service; (e) possess time management ability; (f) exhibit leadership in putting together teams; and (g) use technical writing skills to develop training materials applicable to all skill levels. (Millard, 2006 p. 27)

Our discussion of technology assessment will be limited in scope to the Internet and related workplace technologies and protocols in many ways. First, the reader should adapt information presented in this chapter toward the technology in need of assessment. Next, a gap analysis will need to be conducted in order to more clearly focus the outline of the technology assessment. Following that, the level of diffusion of innovation could be measured and compared on an industry basis. The facilitator needs to acknowledge not only the alignment of current resources with corporate standards, but to also recognize challenges that will exist in the future. Various alternate solutions will need exploration in order to assess risk and mitigate negative consequences. Alternate solutions will need to be benchmarked against other companies with similar problems in order to seek validation. Stakeholder perspectives and possible ethical dilemmas will have to be addressed.

***

Background

Corporations in the 21st century find themselves in a constant struggle to compete for profit and will often times resign themselves to using the lowest common denominator of information technology (IT) and Internet based tools, when in reality they should be striving to create the next common denominator. In this sense most problems with technology are similar and connected to an organization's lack of desire, or inability, to seek out and digest new technologies that can make them more profitable with better service quality.

Technology assessment can be a complex and difficult task. It exists in many different forms under many names. It is a challenge to evaluate, describe, and recommend complex systems using simple language easily understood by managers in the workplace. Technology assessment must also be completed on an ongoing basis with report deadlines that occur quarterly, semi-annually, annually, or in real-time depending on financial resources available for the process. Without assessment, corporations are trapped by constantly investing in new technologies recommended to them by salespersons with no tangible way to assess their return on investment. This often results in money spent on new information technologies without fully integrating existing systems and processes.

The goals of this chapter concerning technology assessment are to help companies recognize their degree of "diffusion of innovation" (DOI), as it relates to use of technology, and to recommend steps toward moving the organization into the ownership stage of adoption. Assessments able to provide documentation to upper management in plain language can help greatly in motivating movement from the trial, to acceptance, to ownership stages of the DOI theory. Companies who achieve the ownership stage in a reasonable period of time stand to benefit greatly by increasing their market share of the global economy we are now all part of. Upper level managers need to realize the need to purchase and implement specialized software applications, data warehousing databases, and qualitative data analysis tools (CAQDAS) such as NVIVO7 from QSR International.

The technology assessment model described here is simple by comparison and borrows its structure and character from various other models found in the literature. Some might refer to it as a derivation of Holland and Skarke's (2002) Business Project Enabled by IT (BPIT), van Wyk's (2002) Strategic Technology Analysis (STA), Control Self-Assessment Workshops (McQuay, 2005), the IT Balanced Scorecard (Leahy, 2006), or from Wall Street analyst reports (Sommer, 2005). Technology assessment can mean many things and may be known by other names including applications management, change management, data management, infrastructure management, IT management, lifecycle management, and quality management, among others. Technically, technology assessment in a corporate setting is now impractical to consider in the context of any one methodology. That is to say, there is no cookie cutter approach or single model to follow. Each technology assessment must be created in a customized fashion and implemented consistently on a regular basis.

Rias J. van Wyk (2002) discusses the search for a fundamental model over the past 40 years. This search began in the early 1960s with the data automation phenomenon and basic trends in technology development; passed through the 1970s signified by research concerning "systems theory of technology" and "living systems;" proceeded into the 1980s with a revival in the field of "management of technology" and related writings on the "functional approach to technology," "technometrics," "metatechnology," and "a theory of technology;" and continued into the 1990s with additional creative unifying concepts including "theoretical technology" and "technocology" (p. 17). Some current models of technology assessment include technology roadmapping, technology forecasting, IT governance, strategic technology scanning, and strategic technology analysis (STA) among others.

Assessing and Anticipating Business Technology Needs

Assessing and anticipating business technology needs can be a daunting task due to the complexity of technology in the workplace. Key to this component of the SPELIT model will be the identification of a variety of methods to choose from in order to customize a Technology assessment model that uses simple language to easily communicate to the CIO or CEO of the organization. After the problem is firmly identified, then a strategy for assessment can be formulated, taking into consideration the relevant systems, stakeholders, and technology drivers of the organization.

There are many factors to take into consideration when performing a technology assessment.

1) The assessment needs to speak to current operational and future strategic goals;
2) The assessment should offer general guidelines to be used, resulting in better strategic alignment of IT infrastructure;
3) It should be viewed as only a point in time assessment that needs to be constantly repeated in order to remain relevant; and
4) The technology assessment should strive to align IT infrastructure with current and future services offered by competing organizations.

Sommer (2005) supports these ideas but cautions in stating:

Alignment is about building a consensus of what IT's priorities should be. But alignment exercises are often flawed, as they require non-IT persons—namely internal users and line-of-business (LOB) leaders—to define the IT agenda (p. 78).

Sommer goes on to imply that before we attempt to deal with assessment we need to first realize the context of technology in the 21st century. We need to better realize not only how to align our current information technology infrastructure with the competitive forces of industry; but also how to be strategically aligned, in preparation for the future, in order for our business to grow and become more profitable within today's global business environment. In this sense, CIO talent and IT assets must be properly leveraged to help accommodate concerns of all stakeholders. In essence, technology in business cannot merely be aligned to compete with other businesses; technology must be leveraged to support operational and strategic objectives and be robust and intuitive enough for all stakeholders to use effectively.

Communication Comprising Perception, Expectations, and Involvement

Our view of technology must be relevant to both information and business in order to be used by employees in the operation of the organization. Technology's relevance to information helps the organization align itself to industry standards for the sake of efficiency, while its relevance to business lies in its ability to be leveraged for competitive advantage in the marketplace.

In an effort to simplify our assessment of information technology we need to better understand its significance to communication and people. And so it follows that information technology for our purposes will refer to the collection of technologies relevant to the transport of information, knowledge, data, text, audio and video recordings, drawings, and so forth in context to computers, telecommunications, and digital electronics.

Peter Drucker (1958/1970) described the significance of technology to management and society in a series of essays written over 35 years ago, before the advent of the personal computer that will help us to better visualize the framework of our assessment model. Surprisingly, many of his original observations are still relevant today. In his essay entitled "Information, Communications, and Understanding," Drucker asserts four fundamentals of communication that are relevant today in our age of information technology. These fundamentals stress that (1) communication is perception; (2) communication is expectation; (3) communication is involvement; and (4) that communication and information are totally different concepts (p. 4). The following discussion is provided to highlight the importance of effective communication concerning the results of our technology assessment model.

Communication as Perception Related to Technology Assessment

Viewing communication as perception means the recipient or stakeholder is the actual communicator signified by his or her understanding of the information being communicated. The supposed communicator is actually making it possible or impossible for the recipient to perceive and acknowledge that a communication has been made. This is important for our assessment because our stakeholders will get confused if we use jargon that is too technical. We need to identify our stakeholders and formulate a model that uses vocabulary everyone can understand.

Perception further supports this thought in that stakeholders will only derive meaning from the total system that serves as a context for communication. In this sense we want to be careful not to overemphasize vocabulary from the domain of any particular stakeholder at the expense of another. Ideally, we must make sure the language used is more generalized, as if we were preparing a report for the CEO or CIO, being careful to talk to stakeholders in terms of their own experience. If we write at this level of communication we can be sure that stakeholders not only understand the information but also relate to it well. More specifically, we need to be able to produce a report to the CEO or CIO who can in turn clearly communicate findings to all stakeholders.

Communication as Expectation Related to Technology Assessment

With regard to expectations, our technology assessment model must make observations within the domain of what is expected by the shareholders, whether the expectations are negative or positive, while being careful to avoid forcing the stakeholders to realize the unexpected. What this means is that the process in itself should be the learning experience. There should be no surprises in the conclusions and recommendations. Change, especially in context to technology, must occur gradually, if it is to gain any permanence in the workplace. Here, we need to be careful to prepare our stakeholders by always legitimizing our observations with references to real life situations using a combination of benchmarking, gap analysis, needs assessment, and strategic thinking. In this way, we can be sure to communicate in terms that utilize the reader's expectations. We want the reader to understand our recommendations as opposed to hearing our recommendation with an accompanied nod from time to time, while yielding no measurable change in performance.

Communication as Involvement Related to Technology Assessment

Here, we can leverage the use of surveys by creating not only a means to gather information from stakeholders, but to also teach stakeholders through involvement with the survey. Survey questions can be formulated to show connections to other areas of technology within the company, allowing the respondent to think outside the box of his or her normal work setting. In other words, a survey must be created in a way that stakeholders can reflect on enterprise information needs, as well as corporate performance measures and critical success factors. If stakeholders feel involved, they are more apt to be receptive to not only providing realistic and accurate recommendations, but to also follow them in the future.

Communication and Information as Different but Related

Communication and information are totally different for obvious reasons, but related in the sense that data (information), on its own, cannot be understood without a context; and that context must be communicated. Since the context of data, and raw data are inseparable to human understanding, communication then becomes an integral part of data yet separate from it at the same time. This argument is also relevant to the survey portion of our assessment since each question asked should have a context that shows connections to other areas of technology.

***

Technology Assessment: Methodology Framework Considerations

Technology assessment as it applies to business can mean many things. Kaczmarek (2006) defines technology assessment (TA) as a process of reviewing new and emerging technologies to determine potential benefits and risks to a particular organization and basing purchasing decisions on those findings. However, we must concern ourselves with more than just purchasing. Our assessment must prepare our organization for the challenges of the 21st century. We need to manage, update, or develop systems that meet the 21st century information needs of our organization by asking many questions, including whether or not to keep or replace our existing systems.

Our basic framework for assessment will be in context to internal and external technology drivers, how they affect our current level of service, and how they can be leveraged to better prepare for the future. In order to accomplish this, our assessment model must address up to five system components as well as the variety of stakeholders within each system in addition to consideration of newer technologies.

Understanding Technology System Components

Five systems in need of consideration as part of a basic framework for environmental analysis include IS (information systems), IT (information technology), TPS (transaction processing systems), MIS (management information systems), and DSS (decision-support systems). Please refer to Appendix 9A for an explanation of technology system terminology. A careful evaluation taking into account each system will better ensure the accuracy of information.

Acknowledging Technology Stakeholders

Stakeholders, or information workers, will vary from one organization to the next, but are generally categorized as system owners, internal and external system users, system designers, system builders, and system analysts. Please refer to Appendix 9B for an explanation of stakeholder terminology. Here, it is important to realize that all these categories are made up of people, each with their own "silent language" comprising not only environment, tone of voice, and mannerisms, but also cultural and organizational factors stemming from past social, political, economic, legal, inter-cultural , and technological experiences. (Hall, 1959/1970). Ideally, we need to form a team comprising at least two members from each category, but for our purposes we should survey as many members as possible and process the results.

Newer Technologies as Business Technology Drivers

Business and technology drivers of different systems may vary accordingly. Nonetheless, internal drivers could include (a) networks and the Internet; (b) mobile and wireless technologies; and (c) enterprise applications, security, and privacy. External drivers include (a) business process design and knowledge management; (b) collaborative technologies and a cycle of continuous improvement; (c) electronic commerce and e-business; (d) partnership and collaboration; and (e) globalization and outsourcing.

Newer technologies specifically related to the Internet and its many protocols include very high-level "human oriented" languages (VHLL) such as DHTML (Dynamic Hypertext Markup Language), XML (Extensible Markup Language), SMIL (Synchronized Multimedia Integration Language), WML (Wireless Markup Language), and XBRL (Extensible Business Reporting Language); scripting languages such as ASP (Active Server Pages), JavaScript, Python, REBOL (Relative Expression-Based Object Language); and Tcl (Tool Command Language); and high-level task oriented languages such as Perl (Practical Extraction and Reporting Language), Java, and Cold Fusion.

Other technologies used over networks and the Internet include intranets, extranets, portals, and reusable web services in addition to mobile and wireless technologies comprised of handheld computers or PDA's, cell phones, integrated devices (comprising cell phones and PDA's); supporting technologies such as Bluetooth, WiFi, and a note 802.11; collaborative technologies such Microsoft's Live Meeting, Webex's PCNow and WebOffice, Raindance's meeting, seminar, and conferencing solution, and Saba's Centra Live software; and a core set of enterprise applications.

End-State Goals of Technology Assessment

The importance of any technology assessment lies in its ability to help the CEO or CIO generate new ideas and to be able to communicate those ideas using documentation that is easily understood by the CEO or CIO. In our case, we need to seek out and identify assimilation gaps in addition to tracking future technologies so the CEO or CIO can make decisions ensuring increased profitability and higher levels of service quality. These ideas are generated systematically and can be framed by four main goals including:

1) Characterizing current corporate technological conditions as well as identifying the business driver(s) used as a context for technology assessment;
2) Create a taxonomy and map the technological landscape leading to the recognition of internal strengths and weaknesses;
3) Articulate the challenges that exist, leading to benchmarking other highly successful companies; and
4) Identify external opportunities and threats to, not only noting opportunities that may exist, but to also leveraging new technologies to increase efficiency, yielding greater profitability and service quality.

A framework is necessary to produce a report in context to the business drivers (described below) in today's corporate environment. These drivers include business process redesign of legacy applications, collaboration and partnership with other corporate entities, corporate alignment with globalization of the economy, electronic commerce and business, security and privacy, knowledge asset management, or continued improvement through a total quality management process. Once a business driver has been chosen, a taxonomy of categories related to the driver must be developed.

We will focus on procedures in place, supporting areas within security and privacy, and needed software quality improvements for the purposes of our discussion. Our survey will have to be designed, asking questions pertaining to two levels. The first should assess our current implementation of technology to measure how we align to other industry standards used as a benchmark. The second should address software quality improvements to be made in a strategic effort to compete in the future. With regard to the first level, a taxonomy of 14 departments to survey as part of our report for a fictitious organization that I will call the ABC Company has been adapted from a security policy template found in Cronkhite and McCullough's (2001) book entitled *Access Denied: The Complete Guide to Protecting Your Business Online*. In addition, information from a second taxonomy, addressing software quality improvements, has been added to our original (Howey, 2002). These taxonomies are only relevant to this writing. Other taxonomies may need to be adopted, adapted, or newly created to assess other business technology drivers mentioned previously.

After combining both taxonomies as a template, you will need to put together an assessment team of individuals; each familiar with the technology area they are assigned. Each member will create, facilitate, and process a survey for each of the 14 technology areas outlined in Appendix 9A. This survey would ask for specific answers to questions related to the following end-state goals mentioned above in addition to proposing a tangible means of assessment that is accepted by the industry to enable benchmarking with other organizations' IT Internet-based technologies. Questions asked in the survey would also need to include moral dimensions and inverse relationships that may exist, such as the relationship between security and privacy (e.g., more security results in less privacy).

The design of our technology assessment will be adapted from a combination of other assessment models found in current literature. This technology assessment will involve an examination of stakeholder perceptions concerning more than the current quality of hardware, software, and procedural services offered by the organization. It will need to measure the degree to which company resources align to industry standards in addition to promoting new systems and procedures leading to greater efficiency, profit, and service quality. According to Sommer (2005), "To be strategic, companies and their leaders must be innovative, calculated risk takers. Risk-taking, as opposed to order taking, should be a strategic competency for the CEO" (p. 80).

Purpose of the Assessment

Although an assessment of this type may aid the stakeholders in different ways, the main purpose of the technology assessment will be to help the CEO or CIO to formulate a strategy to help employees in the organization being assessed to move forward into the ownership stage of what Everett Rogers refers to as the "diffusion of innovation" (Rogers, 1995). The design of this technology assessment must use interpretations in such a way as to address the common problem of "diffusion of innovation," making recommendations aiding the company's full transition into the ownership stage. Essentially, the focus of this technology assessment will be to spotlight employees and their relationship to technology. Holland and Skarke (2002) support this intent by pointing out that only 20% of companies find their way to the ownership stage in which the operation of business leverages technology as an asset to further increase market share. Holland and Skarke further discuss "diffusion of innovation" in three stages including trial, acceptance, and ownership, in context to trust, leadership, and measurement; also taking into account the many taxonomies of technological infrastructure in the workplace. In the trial stage, businesses will strive to understand how information technology (IT) might work. In this sense, IT leads the way, often times with substantial cost but low value potential. In the acceptance stage, IT is substituted as a more effective and efficient means of conducting business. IT leads the business side, with cost savings and moderate value potential. In the last stage, ownership, IT is exploited as another business asset with the business side leading IT, and is measured in context to its return on investment (ROI) with a high value potential.

The remainder of this paper will include additional discussion regarding the technology assessment design, purpose of the assessment, and research questions, followed by information describing the survey instrument. The end of this chapter deals with procedures for data collection, preparation, and findings based upon analysis of the data, followed by a summary to prepare the reader for findings of the study, conclusions, and recommendations.

Technology Assessment Design

Conducting a technology assessment can be a complicated and daunting task, due to the hierarchical and complex relationship between various systems and subsystems, resulting in a report that is of little use to anyone unless it is carefully planned, outlined, and executed. Its scope must be limited to the use and effectiveness of technologies in context to the size of the organization. Size will obviously dictate the type of technology used to form information systems capable of obtaining and organizing data into useful information. Partners, employees, suppliers, and customers may all require a specific enterprise application in combination with hardware and categorized according to the functions they serve. All of these systems will have to be accounted for by developing a taxonomy of relationships between the technology systems used in the organization; similar to how Van Wyk (2002) speaks to developing a taxonomy in context to a fundamental framework called strategic technology analysis (STA). STA is an important model to consider because it focuses on the intrinsic characteristics of technologies in context to the anatomy, taxonomy, evolution, and ecology of technology in the workplace. We're striving to accomplish similar goals with a slightly different focus on a strategic plan for the future. After a taxonomy of relationships has been established, an outline can be formulated in preparation for the survey instrument.

***

Data Collection, Preparation, and Findings

The survey for each department's data collection should be web based and XML compliant, posted online for employees to use, and delivered via specialized browser-based software on the secure company intranet. All employees should be required to answer all questions within a reasonable length of time and then be able to change any of their answers at any time after the initial deadline. In this way, employees could update their surveys on a quarterly or annual basis (hard deadline) with the option of changing their answers at any time in order to generate new data sets leading to better computer-assisted analysis, and constant improvement of recommendations. Survey questions should not only seek out responses but also teach employees about connections to other departments and procedures they may not be aware of.

The facilitator of the technology assessment should assemble managers from all departments of the company and should consult with the managers to gain approval of questions used in the survey instrument as they relate to our taxonomy discussed earlier. The questions posed should be aligned to the procedures of each individual department and should request employees to answer no more than four or five questions per day with a hard deadline for all questions to be answered. A specific description of the survey instrument, in addition to a question bank offered as an example of the types of questions to ask, can be found in Appendix 9B.

Data could then be analyzed using specialized computer-assisted qualitative data analysis tools (CAQDAS) such as XSight and NVIVO7 from (among others):

- QSR International (http://www.qsrinternational.com/),
- ATLAS.ti (http://www.atlasti.de/),
- HyperRESEARCH (http://www.researchware.com/),
- MAXqda (http://www.maxqda.de/),
- QDAMiner (http://www.provalisresearch.com/),
- Qualrus (http://www.ideaworks.com/news.shtml), and
- Transana (http://www.transana.org/).

Each of the software solutions recommended above have their own strengths and levels of complexity. The facilitator would be wise to either carefully choose and use one of them or hire an additional consultant to code and process the collected data. These programs should serve only as tools to track, organize, and process data in preparation for analysis by a human who can then provide conclusions and recommendations. A more detailed analysis of features from each program can be found in a working paper at http://caqdas.soc.surrey.ac.uk entitled "Choosing a CAQDAS Software Package 4th Edition" (Lewins & Silver, 2006).

Conclusions and Recommendations

Our technology component of the SPELIT framework responds to research suggesting limitations to increasing business value are no longer technological but social. As additional funds are spent to facilitate learning processes, future employees will need to learn to leverage technology to help their prospective companies be more efficient and cost effective, able to remain highly competitive and capture greater market share. Companies are evolving out of the trial stage of developing or maintaining a technological infrastructure and into acceptance of the idea that technological infrastructure will soon no longer be an issue as specialized business software evolves into secure web-based groupware. Barry Levine (2006) in his article concerning Web 2.0, states the following:

> The Internet is evolving. Whereas once it served mostly as a conduit for data, today the World Wide Web is turning into something more akin to a giant operating system, an immense interactive platform on which full-blown applications run in your browser and collaboration occurs in real time. (para 1)

In this sense companies are now ready to own the various technologies in the work place by focusing on training. Unfortunately, there are still social limitations causing an alignment gap between the introduction of technology and effective use of it in the workplace to the extent that most corporations are still having trouble (Holland & Skarke, 2002). Capellà (2005) further supports the need to close the alignment gap by discussing survey results of CIOs and CFOs of global 3000 companies conducted in September and October of 2005:

> While the pressure to maintain IT operational efficiency has certainly not subsided, CIOs report a renewed emphasis—and increased funding—for growth-enabling projects. These include streamlining supply chains, upgrading customer-relationship management capabilities, and expediting collaboration across the extended enterprise. (p. 78)

There are also legislative issues, such as Network Neutrality and Internet Neutrality that could either jump-start or bog-down an evolution to a more centralized online business software model. More importantly, the growth initiatives mentioned above will all require specialized software and supporting hardware infrastructure (onsite or on the Internet) to be learned by all employees on a continuous basis, starting the cycle of diffusion of innovation over again. Online business application software, such as NetSuite (see http://www.netsuite.com/portal/products/netsuite/main.shtml?promocode=nf_14) is an example.

Technology assessment will therefore have to be continually facilitated, updated, and presented on at least an annual basis in the context of a strategic plan whose objectives are passed down from the CEO or CIO to managers and their prospective departments. A continuous cycle of technology assessment and improvement must be in place as a kind of risk assessment process in order to mitigate problems caused by future economic volatility and technology advancement. Responses to the results of survey information could be made by documenting observations or concerns and making recommendations in the form of an actionable fix for each item (in a manner that can be measured for accountability purposes).

In addition, current technological advances, such as the significance of XBRL and XML, must be accounted for and balanced against other competing factors. Such factors include constraints on human and financial resources, corporate market saturation, service branding, and ensuring a measurable return on investment, in addition to ethical and legal considerations.

***

Summary

In conclusion, the final stages of our technology assessment will include a rough draft report of the findings, a focus-group discussion, and the presentation and submission of a final position paper to be given to the CEO or CIO of the company on a quarterly or yearly basis. The organization of the position paper should follow a structure adapted from the taxonomy found in Appendix 9A to produce fourteen separate reports that can later be combined and summarized.

The next chapter will discuss the other possible environments of a SPELIT analysis.

***

References

Capellà, J. M. (2005). Closing the alignment gap [It still exists]. *Optimize*, *4*(11), 77.

Cronkhite, C., & McCullough, J. (2001). *Access Denied*. Berkeley, California: Osborne/McGraw-Hill.

Digby, C., & Harji, S. (2006, February 26). How can your IT make or break the deal. *Computer Weekly*, 30.

Drucker, P. (1970). *Technology, Management, and Society*. New York: Harper and Row Publishing. (Original work published 1958)

Gay, L. R. (1992). *Educational Research: Competencies for Analysis and Application* (4th ed.). New York: MacMillan Publishing.

Hall, E. T. (1970). *The Silent Language*. New York: Anchor Books. (Original work published 1959)

Holland, D., & Skarke, G. (June 2002). Jump to the next level of IT productivity. *Hydrocarbon Processing*, 87-90.

Howey, R. A. (Fall 2002). Understanding software technology. *Knowledge, Technology, and Policy*, 15(3), 70-71.

Kaczmarek, D. (2006, May). Best practice: Getting a handle on technology. *Healthcare Purchasing News*, 30(5), 68.

Leahy, T. (April 2006). Instilling a BPM mind-set into IT practices. *Business Finance*, 12(4), 43-46.

Levine, B. (2006, June 30). Unlocking the Promise of Web 2.0. *Newfactor Magazine Online*. Retrieved June 30, 2006, from Newsfactor Magazine Online Web site: http://www.newsfactor.com/story.xhtml?story_id=13200003GDTC

Lewins, A., & Silver, C. (2006). *Choosing a CAQDAS Software Package 4th Edition* (Retrieved from http://caqdas.soc.surrey.ac.uk/). London: University of London.

Macer, T. (2005, December). XSight 1.2 [Review of the software]. *Quirk's Marketing Research Review*. Retrieved June 16, 2006, from http://www.qsrinternational.com/ Web site: http://www.qsrinternational.com/products/productoverview/XSight.htm

McNally, A. (January 2006). Taking the guesswork out of customer satisfaction. *Food Management*, 41(1), 2026.

McQuay, P. (December 2005). Systems development audits. *The Internal Auditor, 62*(6), 58-62.

Millard, E. (2006, May 26). Getting it down to business: IT talent is still important, but business skills are in increasing demand, two. *Processor, 28*(21), 27.

Ohmae, K. (2000). *The invisible continent: Four strategic imperatives of the new economy.* New York: Harper-Collins Publishers Inc.

Rogers, E. M. (1995). *Diffusion of Innovations.* New York: The Free Press.

Sommer, B. (2005). Stop aligning, take risks! *Optimize, 4*(12), 78.

The Woodrow Wilson School of Public, & International Affairs. (1995). *Technology assessment and the work of congress* (Agency Archive). Washington, DC: Princeton University. Retrieved June 17, 2006, from www.wws.princeton.edu Web site: http://www.wws.princeton.edu/ota/ns20/proces_f.html

van Wyk, R. J. (Fall 2002). Technology: A fundamental structure. *Knowledge, Technology and Policy, 15*(3), 1435.

Appendix 9A
Technology System Component Terminology

IS (Information Systems)

Pronounced as separate letters, and short for *information systems* or *information services*. For many companies, IS is the name of the department responsible for computers, networking, and data management. Other companies refer to the department as *IT* (Information Technology) and *MIS* (Management Information Services) (http://www.webopedia. com/, p. 1).

Information Technology (IT)

Short for *information technology*, and pronounced as separate letters, the broad subject concerned with all aspects of managing and processing information, especially within a large organization or company. Because computers are central to information management, computer departments within companies and universities are often called *IT departments*. Some companies refer to this department as *IS (information services)* or *MIS (management information services)* (http://www.webopedia.com/, p. 1)

Transaction Processing System (TPS)

A type of computer processing in which the computer responds immediately to user requests. Each request is considered to be a *transaction*. Automatic teller machines for banks are an example of transaction processing (http://www.webopedia.com/, p. 1).

Management Information System (MIS)

Short for *management information system* or *management information services*, and pronounced as separate letters, MIS refers broadly to a computer-based system that provides managers with the tools for organizing, evaluating, and efficiently running their departments. In order to provide past, present, and prediction information, an MIS can include software that helps in decision making, data resources such as databases, the hardware resources of a system, decision support systems, people management and project management applications, and any computerized processes that enable the department to run efficiently (http://www.webopedia.com/, p. 1).

Decision-Support System (DSS)

Abbreviated *DSS*, the term refers to an interactive computerized system that gathers and presents data from a wide range of sources, typically for business purposes. DSS applications are systems and subsystems that help people make decisions based on data that is culled from a wide range of sources (http://www.webopedia.com/, p. 1).

Appendix 9B
Survey Instrument

The design of the survey instrument should be made in the spirit of shared participative decision-making amongst employees from different divisions of the company. That is to say, two managers from each of the 14 units assessed need to be responsible for facilitating the survey, collecting information, and preparing a report to be submitted to the designated consultant or project-management leader. One manager will use a survey to collect data from front line managers and users of information services, while the other uses a survey to collect data related to the operation of business units. Both surveys will ask questions focused on operational aspects needed for alignment and strategic aspects necessary to go beyond thinking operationally; described by Sommer (2005) as follows:

The focus of operational CIOs should be on (1) creating insights into existing systems, (2) adopting technology to match competitors' capabilities, (3) upgrading technology to cut costs or boost performance, and (4) upgrading technology with little change in functionality. The focus of strategic CIOs should be on (1) locking up new technology to create long-term, competitive block; (2) developing technologies that will dramatically alter the competitive landscape; (3) and forming partnerships to develop new capabilities (p. 80).

The designated consultant or project management leader will then combine all 14 reports into one technology assessment "white paper" to be submitted to the CEO or CIO of the company for further review and action.

The effectiveness of our survey will depend entirely upon the data collected as it relates to preparing for competition and success in the 21st century global economy. Data in need of collection could include e-mail communications, transcripts of virtual meetings, notes from formal meetings, data reports, conversations with stakeholders, as well as previous reports from other stakeholders that may have significance. After collecting materials a survey needs to be created in order to further consider the value of what we have in relation to current and future needs and how those needs can be best served; whether by integrating new systems or replacing old ones. Financial and social aspects must also be considered toward measuring not only money spent in the short term but also money saved in the long term. Current and future information systems and usage procedures must be robust and also intuitive to the user, regardless the level of computer literacy.

Preparing Our Survey Instrument

Preparing a valid survey instrument will be key to the success of our technology assessment. Our instrument could be adopted from a combination of other surveys already known or could be an adaptation of questions from a variety of sources. McNally (2006) suggests three levels of inquiry in context to customer service and business process improvement (BPI) which could relate well to the creation of our technology assessment. She recommends a three-level approach to inquiry including general performance questions, specific service level questions focused on each department, and the use of focus groups to explore the root of problems identified within the written survey.

Questions for our instrument should come from managers of each of the perspective departments and approved by a focus group created for the sole purpose of ensuring question validity to corporate needs. See also McQuay (2005).

The following is a collection of short excerpts from various sources—Digby and Harji (2006), Glasser (2006), and Sommer (2005)—that could be adapted for our purposes to serve as a starting point. Digby and Harji (2006) touch on technology assessment in terms of vendor due diligence as it relates to acquisitions. Eight of 10 key questions asked are related to our technology assessment and include the following:

> Is the technology current?
> How well does the technology support the business?
> Is the functionality fit for purpose?
> Is the technology robust, stable, and resilient?
> Are effective business continuity plans in place?

What are the significant risks and how can they be mitigated?
What are the short and medium-term capital requirements?
Are operational costs sustainable and where can savings be made? (p. 30)

John Glasser (2006, p. 104-108) writes about assessing the IT function in less than one day, and asks a multitude of relevant questions in the areas of infrastructure and applications performance, execution, and alignment. Questions that you might ask include the following:

Re: Infrastructure and applications.
How often does the system go down?
Are there days when the system is very slow?
Are managers aware of any time that the system was brought to its knees by a virus attack?
Do you track downtime-and what do the data tell you?
Are you current with vendor releases?
How do you manage virus protection?
When the infrastructure has problems, what are procedures for responding?

Re: Execution-implementing new applications and supporting users.
Questions in regard to achieving desired outcomes:
Picking three recent implementations, what were the objectives?
To what degree were the objectives achieved?
If the organization fell short in achieving objectives, why did this happen?
Was the implementation on time and on budget?
Did the implementation go relatively smoothly?

Questions in regard to engaging users effectively:
Did the implemented system improve the operation of your department?
Was the training good?
Were the IT group and the vendor responsive to issues and problems?
Was the representation of users effective on various task forces and project teams?

Questions in regard to front-line support:
Does the IT department measure its service? [Describe how.]
Has the IT department established service goals?
Was the organizations management involved in setting those goals?
Does the IT department regularly solicit feedback on its service?

Questions in regard to department liaisons:
Who is your IT liaison, and does the liaison do a good job?
Can you give me some examples of issues that you have raised with the liaison?
Where those issues well resolved?
Does your liaison do a good job of keeping you up-to-date on IT plans?
Do you consider this liaison to be a member of your team?

Re: Alignment—General questions:
Can you take each item in your strategy and performance improvement plans and point to the IT initiatives that support these undertakings?
If there are IT initiatives that cannot be mapped to organizational strategy and plans, could you discuss why you approved these initiatives?
Is there a regular senior leadership discussion of the IT agenda?
Does leadership take responsibility for making decisions about which IT initiatives to find?
Does the CIO take the lead in bringing new information technologies to the attention of the management team?

Questions in regard to governance:
Is the process for setting the IT budget well understood, efficient, sufficiently rigorous, and perceived as fair?
Is there a well-accepted approach for acquiring new applications?
To the IT project teams have well-defined roles and methods for implementing new systems?

Sommer (2005) asks the following questions concerning strategic global strategies and outsourcing:

> [If] effectively half our IT staff is based in India, should we continue to do this in case the dollar devalues?
> If the average retailer has moved 35% more product per employee during the past 5 years, how can we use IT to boost revenue per employee?
> Can our IT group devise a new in-store technology no other company has?
> How can we exploit our superior handling and protection of customers, employees, and supplier data?
> Beyond software code, how can our IT group supplement its business solutions with other content intellectual property to differentiate the company's offerings and assist the sales staff? (p. 82)

Chapter 10
Environmental Epilogue

Leo A. Mallette, Ed.D.
Program Manager

***

Introduction

This short chapter almost didn't exist. It was going to be two or three footnotes in some of the previous six chapters. However, there are many specialized environments that could be part of several of the SPELIT POWER MATRIX environments or could be their own environments. We felt that these other environments were a special topic and should be discussed in their own chapter. This chapter will address other environments (ethical, educational, physical, religious, and security).

Ethical Environment

Ethics can be categorized in the legal environment, although there is a social and intercultural element associated with ethical decisions. You could also argue that there is a political component to the ethical environment.

The official study of ethics is fairly new to the field of business, but it is fast becoming one of the most important considerations. To properly examine business ethics, we need to look at the environment of established values and theories. Two major ethical theories are (a) utilitarianism, which posits that behavior and its outcome should result in the greatest good for the largest number of people, and (b) deontology, or rule-based morality, which focuses on actions, respect for others, and what reasonable people would agree is right. The challenge for organizations today is to balance the need to satisfy their stakeholders' business needs while protecting their employees' desires for privacy (Ferrell, Fraedrich, & Ferrell, 2002) and dignity (Kierkegaard, 2005).

For example, the ethics of monitoring employee e-mail and website usage has become one of the major ethical dilemmas in business today because "electronic surveillance is now the norm and not the exception" (Twarog, 2005, p. 6). The legal precedent regarding e-mail and employee privacy has been set in favor of the company or the government in cases dating back to at least 1990 (Chociey, 1997) and is now the norm. A SPELIT analysis of the ethical environment would have to consider the utilitarian view that their organization needs to monitor employee e-mail and website use is serving the greatest good for the greatest number of people, with employees' deontological views of what is reasonable, which involves protecting the employee's right to privacy.

Educational Environment

The educational environment is often a world unto itself; ask any doctoral student, or someone pursuing a new hobby. From chapter 2, we learned that each adult learner possesses a special set of cognitive abilities, experiences, values, and goals, which allow their full potential to thrive. There also exists a set of shared principles and values that bond together each adult learner. Jacqueline Pritchett used the phrase *The Adult Learner* in order to illustrate the holistic nature present in Andragogy theory. Knowles, et al (1998) identified the following six characteristics that richly describe the adult as learner:

1. Adult learners are self-directed and autonomous.
2. Adult learners possess an array of knowledge through their personal and professional life experiences.
3. Adult learners are goal-oriented in nature.
4. Adult learners are practical.
5. Adult learners are relevancy-oriented.
6. Adult learners should be granted respect and shown it accordingly by their instructors.

Moreover, Knowles, et al (1998) describes the six essential core principles and concepts that energize each adult in the learning environment as follows:

- the learner's need to know
- self-directed learning
- prior experiences of the learner
- readiness to learn
- orientation to learning, and
- motivation to learn (p. 4).

The educational environment could include portions of the social environment (decisions on public schools or home-schooling), the political environment (an assistant professor attempting to gain tenure), or the economic environment (an undergraduate student deciding on working or graduate school). Education and learning is significant part of any adult's life and may be part of a SPELIT environmental analysis. Education can be an environment to analyze in your organization

Physical Environment

The SPELIT technological environment could include the physical environment with basic tools such as shelter (facilities), food distribution channels, and a country's infrastructure or it could be part of the capital goods in the economics environment. Very few organizations exist without a physical environment. It may be centralized like a factory or distributed like the power grid for a country. In many cases, the physical environment must be evaluated independently of the other environments when performing a SPELIT environmental analysis.

Religious or Spiritual Environment

Should the religious environment be part of the intercultural environment? After all, different religions represent different views. In many countries, religion and politics are inextricably mixed. The legal view in the United States separates business and religion. However, many people have a religious belief or are spiritual. The organization you are analyzing may or may not have a religious environment.

In some cases, religious beliefs and practices will not be part of the organization being analyzed and can be ignored. Even though many organizational change (transition) specialists would like to believe this, or believe it has been legislated out of the U.S. government and business workplace, it may still be there.

Employees or suppliers in non-U.S. countries may have different beliefs about the degree of religious involvement in the organization you are analyzing. The organization you are performing a SPELIT environmental scan on may be a religious group or affiliated with a religious group. An example is that some schools have a religious affiliation. Students are required to take religion-related classes and faculty may be required to adhere to certain guidelines. In certain cases, the religious environment must be considered for organizations.

Security Environment

The organization that you are studying may have aspects that are classified or the information may be proprietary for the company. The report you prepare analyzing the SPELIT environment may contain sensitive information. A SPELIT analysis is not an annual report; it is an in-depth review of an organization and the driving forces in the various environments at one point in time. Sometimes identifying a driving force or problem is more than half of the solution. However, knowledge of the driving forces or problems may not be information that a company wants to share with competitors or shareholders or even employees.

The security environment of products may be defined by others outside the organization. A recent article (Beach, 2006) discusses the multiple independent levels of security (MILS) architecture for use by defense contractors and universities. The security of our personal information and money on the internet is becoming a more important issue every day. Similar to the above, there are times when you must consider the security environment.

***

Summary

There are many specialized environments that could be part of several of the SPELIT POWER MATRIX environments or could be their own environments. This chapter addressed the ethical, educational, physical, religious, and security environments.

This concludes Part II of this book and the discussions on the individual environments of the SPELIT analysis method. Part III will provide examples of how the SPELIT method has been used.

***

References

Beach, C. (2006). *Many levels of security*. Retrieved July 25, 2006 at http://

www.military-information-technology.com/print_article.cfm?docid=1537

Chociey, P. A. (1997). Who's Reading My E-Mail?: a Study of Professionals' E-Mail Usage and Privacy Perceptions in the Workplace. *IEEE Transaction on Professional Communication, 40*(1), 34-40.

Ferrell, O., Fraedrich, J., & Ferrell, L. (2002). *Business ethics: Ethical decision making and cases.* Boston, MA: Houghton Mifflin.

Kierkegaard, S. (2005). *Privacy in electronic communication: Watch your e-mail: Your boss is snooping!* Denmark.

Twarog, J. (2005). Internet monitoring at work and employee privacy. *Massachusetts Nurse, 76*(8), 6.

Part III
Applications

Part II discussed the individual environments of the SPELIT POWER MATRIX and Part III provides the reader with ideas of how to think about an organization's environment and some ways to present the SPELIT method outlined in this book.

Chapter 11 will provide a variety of examples with different formats by a variety of practitioners. In chapter 12, MD Haque and J. Yu describe a detailed SPELIT analysis of an organization that demonstrates three major aspects: first, how SPELIT can be applied in an organization to capture different environmental drivers; second, to what extent each driver plays an important role in the organization or what essential drivers are missing from the organizational environments; and third, how negative and positive environmental drivers could be separated and applied to the process of organizational change.

A concluding chapter summarizes the ideas presented in this useful book.

Chapter 11
Applications, Formats & Examples

Leo A. Mallette, Ed.D.

***

Introduction

This chapter provides applications, formats, and examples from many fields in the form of case studies. Many authors have contributed case studies for this chapter and all of the company names have been changed to maintain anonymity. Each case study uses a specific example that was researched by the author as part of what would or did become a transition plan for an individual or organization. Some organizational names were changed to provide anonymity.

The SPELIT analysis method, and predecessor theories (SPEL, S/PEL, SPELT), described in this paper have been used by "mid-career professionals interested in becoming scholar-practitioners who are pursuing the doctorate in Organizational Leadership at a university defined as research intensive within the WASC category" (J. Schmieder-Ramirez, Fortson, & Madjidi, 2004, p. 12).

Many of the case studies use select parts of the SPELIT analysis model as determined by the author. The first two categories are often combined and the analysis methodology is abbreviated S/PELT, as in the first case study that follows. This chapter provides many case studies for your instruction and use. The following formats and case studies are presented in this chapter.

- Driving Forces Format

- Case Study 1   Assessment of the Pasadena Propulsion Center
- Case Study 2   Assessment of the Satellite Design and Development Division of the Big Aerospace Corporation
- Positive and Negative Effects Format
  - Case Study 3   Assessing the SAEC Daisy-Wheel Organization
  - Case Study 4   Assessment of an Educational Non-Profit Organization
- Fishbone Format
  - Graduate School Decision Example

***

Driving Forces Format

There are many ways to present the results of a SPELIT analysis. One popular method is the driving forces format, in which individual driving forces are listed. These driving forces can be bulleted in one box or itemized for each SPELIT topic as shown in Table 11-1. The bulleted version of this format is used for case studies 1 and 2.

Table 11-1
Format for SPELIT Analysis Matrix, Showing Multiple Driving Forces

SPELIT Drivers	Driving Force 1	Driving Force 2	Driving Force 3
Social			
Political			
Economic			
Legal			
Intercultural			
Technological			

***

Case Study 1
Assessment of the Pasadena Propulsion Center (PPC)
Mark Romejko, Task Manager

The subject of this paper is an organization within the Inter-Network Directorate (IND) at the Pasadena Propulsion Center (PPC). The PPC's funding for Fiscal Year 2006 (FY06) has been reduced, and most of the programs will be forced to descope their tasks to remain fiscally responsible.

To accommodate the imposed budget reduction, two organizations within IND, the Operations and Engineering offices, were merged into a single organization that was renamed the Development and Operations Office (DOO). This merger enabled the organization to realize a significant cost savings and remain within the reduced budget, largely due to workforce reductions. I have been selected to lead this new organization.

To get a full appreciation of the state of this new organization, I wanted to perform an environmental scan to determine the answer to the question "Where are we now?" I chose to use the S/PELT Model (J. Schmieder-Ramirez, personal communication, 2004) for my environmental scan, as this model allows for a comprehensive analysis of both internal and external factors that may affect the organization.

Case Study 1 Process

The DOO management team used all of the components of the S/PELT model to determine the factors that may affect the new organization. The process that we used to gather this information was to have each of the managers that reported to me poll their subordinates during group meetings to get grass roots perceptions of some of the drivers that were affecting our organization. These polls were structured in such a way as to elicit responses that could fit into one of the specified categories (i.e., social, political, etc.). The managers reported their findings back to me weekly during our regularly scheduled staff meeting. We also solicited input from our customers as we felt that it was very important to see their view of our organization. Table 11-2 lists some of the findings for each category.

Case Study 1 Summary

The S/PELT model enabled us to look at our organization from strategic points of view and to take corrective actions based upon the feedback that we received. We intend to use the S/PELT model periodically and we see the model as a tool that will enable us to constantly improve our organization.

Table 11-2
Summary of Findings from S/PELT Study of DOO Organization at PPC. (Romejko, 2005)

Element	Findings/Concerns
Social/Political	Neither managers nor employees of the previous organizations had any insight into the process of how the new team was formed. This process has created dissent and unrest and has dramatically reduced morale and productivity
Economic	While there will be an initial savings of approximately $1.9M/year, there are other costs that must be considered. As this is a new organization, the cost of the transition period and learning curve that every new organization goes through should be considered when discussing cost.
Legal	Managers have concerns about potential legal action that may be taken by some of the displaced employees for wrongful termination. One of the older engineers (Joe W.) that had been in the organization was mentioning to a group of his friends that he felt that he was incorrectly chosen to be laid off and that he would pursue legal action if he was terminated.
Technological	Cause for concern that the merged organization does not drop the ball and can be relied upon to maintain the Inter-Network Directorate's technical capability.

The S/PELT model has proven to be an effective process and can be used to assess the status of an organization at any point during its life cycle. S/PELT allows management teams to obtain constructive feedback from both inside as well as outside of the organization in areas that have the greatest impact. The S/PELT model provides the user with focused feedback that can be categorized and prioritized to enable managers to make methodical and incremental improvements in their organizations.

Case Study 2
Assessment of Satellite Design and Development Division of the Big Aerospace Corporation
James R. DellaNeve, Supervisor, BA Corporation

The names of the corporation and the division of the corporation were changed to provide anonymity. The external authoritative industry information that was used for this analysis was properly referenced without direct quotes to the actual firm.

This research project was to consider and analyze organizational change and learning factors for large information technology projects. The thought processes included in the development of the project included:

- Factors for a framework for success such as the importance of vision, team building, and communication.
- An environmental assessment utilizing the SPELIT framework in order to understand these aspects of the project.
- Factors for organizational change and implementation such as change transition theory, organizational learning, and evaluation methods.

Case Study 2 Process and Results

The process consisted of using external references as a source of information for the analysis. A modified version of the SPELIT model was used (Table 11-3). The four elements of the model used were: Social/Political, Economic, and Legal/Ethical.

***

Format for Describing Positive and Negative Effects

Alternatively, opposing driving forces can be juxtaposed for each SPELIT topic where drivers can be organized into strengths and weaknesses, pluses and minuses, pro and con, right and wrong, good and bad, or credits and debits. We chose negative and positive for the example in Table 11-4. Within each cell, the effects can be ranked in order of importance. The bulleted version of this format is used for case study 3, case study 4, and the example in Chapter 2.

Table 11-3
SPEL/T Analysis Tool Showing the Conditions That are Present in the Firm That the Information Technology Project Leader Will Need to Account for.

Environment	Analysis
Social/Political	Defense related business is highly regulated and dependent on congressional funding as well as geo-political factors. Intelligence related deficiencies uncovered in post 9/11 analysis require improved intelligence capabilities. U.S. Defense strategy movement from large scale engagements to smaller more limited wars.
Economic	The commercial satellite market experienced a dramatic downturn in sales from the boom years in the 1990s to 2002 resulting in general industry overcapacity. Drastic cost cutting measures lead to reductions in personnel which resulted in disruptions and quality problems.
Legal/Ethical	The Federal Trade Commission ruled that the firm was in violation of the Clayton Act which forces restrictions on the firm. In addition, the State Department ruled against the firm in disclosing satellite technology information with China, which resulted in further restrictions on the firm's handling of technical data as well as monitoring of ethics training and International Arms Regulations and Trafficking (ITAR) awareness.

***

Case Study 3
Assessing the SAEC Daisy-Wheel Organization
Eugene Anton, Consultant

The Santa Ana Empowerment Corporation's ("SAEC") Daisy-Wheel Organization is federally funded while leveraging local, county, and state funds. The organization utilizes multiple non-profit and government service providers. The organization functions as a service navigator in the center of the "daisy" in the Daisy-Wheel Network Model. The service navigator maximizes resources by centralizing marketing and administrative services.

The primary goal of the organization is to train and assist in the placement for employment of 800 empowerment zone residents per year, or 5,000 of the empowerment zone workforce by 2012. The empowerment zone covers 3.9 square miles of the City of Santa Ana, California. The zone has 55,652 residents, 38% of the population is under 20 years of age, 55% have less than a 9th grade education, and over 55% are below the poverty level.

Table 11-4
Table Format for SPELIT Analysis Tool Showing Negative and Positive Effects

Environment	Negative Effects	Positive Effects
Social	(-) Leaning to work with the staff from the CVA; overcome territory (-) Require to recruit the sponsor university or medical facility	(+) Meeting experts in the fields
Political	(-) Resistance from the entrenched CVA organization	(+) Civic support from the business community
Economic	(-) Initial cost to implement the program	(+) Benefit to community from the increased revenue stream
Legal	(-) Time, effort and cost of creating a tax exempt organization (-) Filing tax returns	(+) Tax exempt status from being a nonprofit organization
Technological	(-) Registration system and security (-) Website and advertising	(+) Registration, security, tourism base infrastructure exists and services can be purchased

After 3 years of operation, the SAEC Board of Directors requested that the organization provide a higher level of service, maintain placement numbers, and prepare for a possible reduction in funding. I used the

SPELIT analysis as a means to build awareness and ownership by the service providers. The analysis was also used as an environmental scan to provide the SAEC Board of Directors with a revised overall strategy and institute best practices to maximize the Daisy-Wheel program's organizational effectiveness.

Case Study 3 Process and Results

The process included at least four methods of data collection: questionnaires, individual and group interviews, observations, and information gathered from organizations' records and reports. Table 11-5 shows a sample of the highlights from the SPELIT analysis.

Case Study 3 Summary

The Daisy-Wheel Organization used the SPELIT model as the third step in performing a situation analysis. It was necessary to first use the Cause & Effect Dispersion Analysis as described by Brassard and Ritter (1994), to focus the stakeholders on the problem, filter out personal interests, and build consensus. A SWOT (Strengths, Weaknesses, Opportunities, and Threats) analysis was then performed to determine and then balance the internal and external environments of the organization. The SPELIT analysis completed the situation analysis by providing a practical model that was comprehensive and understandable by all participants. The environmental scan was a critical piece in completing a successful continuous change project.

***

Case Study 4
Assessment of an Educational Non-Profit Organization
Dr. David Silverberg, Assistant Professor
Schar College of Education, Ashland University

I came back from Africa determined to create an educational non-profit organization to import teacher training and used the SPELIT model to assess my progress. It was the summer of 2003. Tanzania was as beautiful, welcoming, and parched as I was inspired, visionary, and fruitless. Though SPELIT I saw the power of economic drivers and, thereby, saved my financial assets.

Table 11-5
Case Study 3 Highlights. Last Column (*) Uses 1 to 10 (low to high) for Order of Priority if Action is Required and Level of Ability to Effect Change.

Environment	Main Issues	+/-	Action Steps	*
Social	Poverty	-	Revise strategy, best practices	10
	Lack of education	-	Outreach, family education	8
	Community commitment	+	Leverage local, county and state resources to achieve $1 for $10	10
	Resources	+	Revise SAEC role	7
Political	Formal	+	Petition for additional funding	5
	Political	+ -	Turf battles, reduce money grab	8
	Personal	+ -	Call in favors and make issues public	8
Economic	Unemployment	-	Focus training on growth areas	9
	Lack of transportation	-	Develop alternatives	7
	Business base	+	Survey business needs	8
	Ripple effect	+ -	80% earned in zone stays	-
Legal	Federal restrictions	+ -	Maintain relationship with HUD	10
	Local restrictions	-	Change codes listed in attachment	9
	Multi-level agreements & contracts	+ -	Cross check for consistency	7
	Formal procedures	-	Educate all involved	6
Intercultural	Diversity	+ -	Cultural awareness training	5
	Mistrust	-	Outreach to neighborhood level	8
	Cultural differences	-	Educate on benefits & procedures	8
Technology	Resources	+ -	Share with service providers	10
	Knowledge	-	Workshops and step-by-step	7
	Comfort level	-	Force usage	6

Case Study 4 Process and Results

My process included interviews with Tanzanian civilians, educators, and business people as well as American non-profits, fund raisers, educators, and students. The results were overwhelming: this was a needed service, but there would be significant administrative challenges. Social considerations included the ability to account for cultural differences, language differences, and varying educational needs, both between the United States and Tanzania as well was between different parts of Tanzania itself. Political considerations involved the receptivity, efficacy, and reliability of regional and national governmental bodies as well as the desire to enlist passive or active support of the United States, United Nations, and UNESCO. Economic considerations focused mostly on how to fund this start-up non-profit through grants and gifts. Legal considerations emphasized the acquisition of appropriate non-profit status, thereby clearing the way for donations. Intercultural considerations focused on the need to attune teacher training modules to real-world needs. Technological considerations included the development of a web identity for the project (www.teachtheworld.org) as well as the prospect of web-based instruction modules.

Progress was made in all areas, but it was my unwavering attention to economic realities that caused me to revise my vision for the project. As a start-up venture, I invested my own capital in the hope of building enough momentum to carry me over the proverbial "hump" of the initial phase. Through this process I learned about the substantial wait time that often exists between the cultivation of funding sources and the maturation of funds.

Case Study 4 Summary

I used the SPELIT model to provide assessment of my Teach The World non-profit venture (Table 11-6). In the end, it was this model that helped me appreciate the near-achievement of my dream and informed my decision to terminate the project due to a lack of funds.

***

Fishbone Format

The fishbone diagram is often used as a brainstorming tool by failure analysis teams to capture ideas (without evaluation of the value of the ideas). A fishbone diagram

> is an analysis tool that provides a systematic way to observe cause and effect. The diagram design resembles the skeleton of a fish. Dr. Kaoru Ishikawa, a Japanese quality control statistician from Tokyo University, invented the fishbone diagram in 1943, so a fishbone diagram is sometimes referred to as an *Ishikawa Diagram*. (Geisen, Evans, Mallette, & Suwandee, 2005, p. 10)

An example of a partially completed fishbone tool is provided in Figure 11-1 and in the organizational example in chapter 12.

Table 11-6
Case Study 4 Table Format for SPELIT Analysis Tool Showing Negative and Positive Effects

Environment	Negative Considerations	Positive Considerations
Social Drivers	(-) Challenge of attunement to local needs	(+) Need for Teacher Training
Political Drivers	(-) Acquisition of practical endorsement	(+) Philosophical support
Economic Drivers	(-) Time needed to garner funding	(+) Funding potential
Legal Drivers	(-) Learning curve regarding taxes	(+) Non-profit status
Intercultural Drivers	(-) Reticence of Americans funding sources	(+) Attunement to local needs
Technology Drivers	(-) Technological divide between the United States and Tanzania	(+) Development of web identity for project (www.Teachtheworld.org)

***

Summary

This chapter provided several case studies of the use of the SPELIT POWER MATRIX and provided different formats that can be adapted to your particular organization or situation. The user might consider weighting the criteria, or arranging particularly difficult problems within an environment in a Pareto diagram.

***

References

Geisen, C., Evans, L., Mallette, L. A., & Suwandee, A. (2005). *Organizational analysis tools to identify possible cause and corrective* action for lack of collaboration between principals in a private school. Paper presented at the Hawaii International Conference on Education, Honolulu HI.

Romejko, M. A. (2005). *A Post-Merger Transition Plan for a Technical Organization at the Pasadena Propulsion Center (PPC):A Comprehensive Exam Presented to the Faculty of The Graduate School of Education and Psychology Pepperdine University.* Unpublished manuscript, Culver City.

Schmieder-Ramirez. (2004). Class Lecture.

Schmieder-Ramirez, J., Fortson, J. L., & Madjidi, F. (2004). Assessment of intercultural sensitivity of organizational leadership doctoral students utilizing the intercultural development inventory (IDI). *Scholar and Educator, the Journal of the Society of Educators and Scholars, 26*(1).

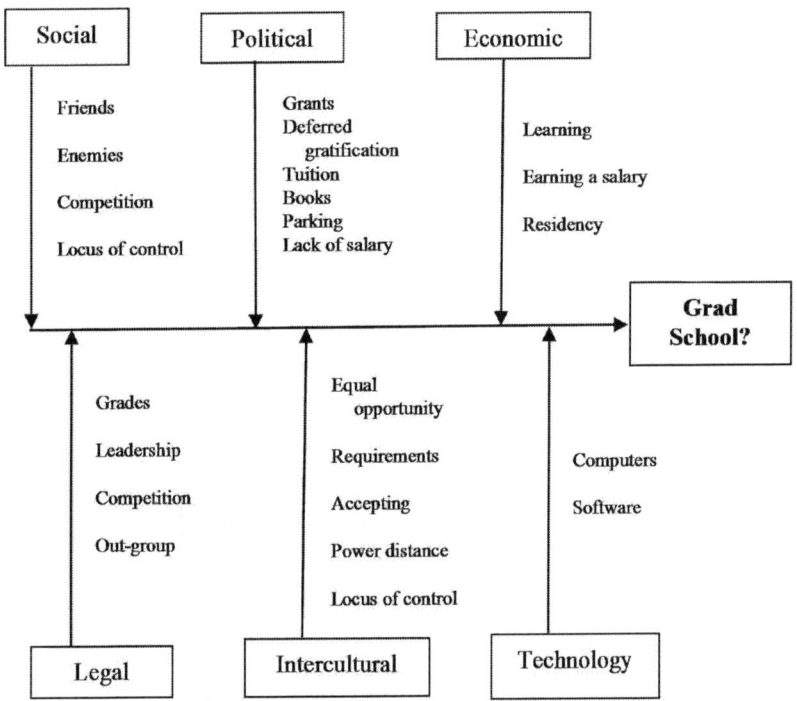

Figure 11-1. SPELIT Analysis Fishbone Diagram. Sample Driving Forces for an Undergraduate's Decision to go to Graduate School.

Chapter 12
An Organizational Example

Main author: MD Mahbubul Haque
Co-author: Joseph Wai Yu

***

Introduction

Headquartered in Southern California, ABC Publications Inc. (a fictitious company) is a leading publishing company concerned about growing competition. The company leaders have expressed anxiety about the preparedness of the company to deal with this challenge. They underlined the immediate needs for developing a felicitous strategy that would enable the company to achieve its mission of staying competitive and retaining its market share. The management wants to deal with this concern in two steps. First, it needs to learn how effectively each division of the organization is functioning and identify the issues that may indicate symptoms of strategic misalignments between the company's mission and the actions being pursued to accomplish the mission. Second, based on the findings, it needs to develop appropriate strategies to amplify proper alignments. By pursuing an environmental scanning, the company could accomplish the first objective, which will ultimately enable them to proceed to the second step. Albright (2004) suggested, "Because of rapid changes in today's marketplace and new and emerging business practices, it is easy for an organization to fall behind by not keeping up in areas such as technology, regulations, and various rising trends. Environmental scanning reduces the chance of being blindsided and results in greater anticipatory management" (p. 40). The SPELIT POWER MATRIX has the strength of performing a thorough environmental analysis by deciphering the social, political, economical, legal, intercultural, and technological areas. Apparently, SPELIT incorporates the six major areas that encompass a typical organizational environment. SPELIT would provide indication of where the company stands in regards to its six major environmental factors so that the company can make strategies accordingly. To be precise, SPELIT will demonstrate where the company stands in its path of attaining its mission.

***

Applying SPELIT in ABC Publications Inc.

Every organization is driven by some critical tasks and attributes that influence its strategic directions. Some researchers and practitioners call them *critical success factors* (Keck et al., 1995), while to many they are known as the *driving factors* (Tregoe et al., 1990). SPELIT analyses will be employed at ABC Publications Inc. to assess its environment in order to perceive the significant driving forces. Both the external and internal environments of the organization will be analyzed, since the organization is affected by the factors emanating from both external and internal environment.

Let's assume that the employees at ABC publications Inc. were invited to participate in a study to identify the driving forces for each of the six factors by using SPELIT in three stages. In the first stage, the participants will be asked to participate in a study in which they will be identifying the driving forces for each of the six types of environment, namely social, political, economic, legal, intercultural, and technological. The study will begin with each participant being asked to prepare a list driving forces for each of the six different environments in the organization. The list will then be tabulated and the drivers with the highest number of appearances will be identified. In order to help the participants to identify the driving forces, the facilitator needs to conduct a debriefing session prior to the start of the actual process, in which a few questions could be asked to make the notion of driving forces comprehensible for the participants. For example, to help stimulate the participants' thoughts to derive the organizational social driver, the facilitator could raise the following questions: what is the corporate culture? What is the teamwork pattern? How are the working relationships? How does information flow from one department to another department? Does the job provide learning and satisfaction? Does management involve workers in their decision making? Is there job security? Is this a fun place to work? Is this a union shop?

For each environment, a different set of questions can be used to facilitate the discovery of the drivers.

Let's assume that the study involves 100 employees from ABC Publications Inc. in which each participant would be asked to identify five drivers from each of the organizational environments. From the list of 500 responses, with 100 in each column, the top five responses with the greatest number of appearances from each of the environments would be identified and placed in Table 12-1.

Table 12-1
Showing Multiple Driving Forces

SPELIT Drivers	Driving Force 1	Driving Force 2	Driving Force 3	Driving Force 4	Driving Force 5
Social	Leadership style	Communication style	Social gathering to boost morale	Teamwork	Corporate structure
Political	Authority & power structure	Conflict Resolution	Resource allocation	Coalition and interest group	Law & regulation
Economic	Economic indices that impact consumption	Global competition increases demand on education	Focused marketing effort to increase consumption	Increase operation efficiency and lower employee turnover	Cost structure of supply chain
Legal	Ethical code of conducts	Government regulations	Intellectual property law	Compliance	Labor law and employee protection
Intercultural	Publishing for diverse communities	Concern for minority opinion	Respect towards other culture	Capturing global customers	Building a diverse workforce
Technological	Efficient technology	Online order processing	Technical assistance	Transportation and communication	funding

In the second stage, the participants would be asked to place each of the driving forces into a "position table" (Table 12-2). The position table entails four quadrants, each designed to rank and position the driving forces into four categories, namely, important and visible, important but not visible, not important but visible, and not important and not visible. Quadrant I shows what driving forces the participants perceive as important and visible or existing within the organizational culture and strategic directions. Quadrant II shows the important forces that the participants do not find missing from the organizational functions. On the other hand, quadrant III shows the driving forces that participants do not consider important but find visible. Quadrant IV exhibits the driving factors that the participants consider to be not important and not visible in the organization. The visibility of a driving factor depends on how the participants perceive it to be embedded in its culture, process, or strategies.

Table 12-2
Position Table

		I Visible	**II** Not Visible
Important	S	Leadership style, Communication style, Social gathering to boost morale, Teamwork, Corporate structure	
	P	Authority & power structure, Conflict Resolution, Resource allocation, Coalition and interest group	Law & regulation
	E	Economic indices that impact consumption, Focused marketing effort to increase consumption	Global competition increases demand on education, Increase operation efficiency and lower employee turnover, Cost structure of supply chain
	L	Ethical code of conducts, Government regulations, Intellectual property law, Compliance	Labor law and employee protection
	I	Publishing for diverse communities, Capturing global customers	Respect towards other culture, Building a diverse workforce
	T	Efficient technology, Online order processing	Technical assistance, Transportation and communication, funding
Not Important	S		
	P		
	E		
	L		
	I		Concern for minority opinion
	T		
		III	**IV**

Each participant would be asked to place the five driving forces in the position table. Let's assume that Table 12-2 shows how one participant positioned the driving forces into each of the quadrants. In analyzing the table, the ideal situation would be quadrant I, which demonstrates that the organization possesses the things that it deems to be important. Quadrant II reveals the concerning factors. To be more precise, the factors located in quadrant II in most cases demonstrate the important drivers that are not discernible within the organizational environments. Apparently, when the organization considers that something is important but the employees do not perceive that to be visible, it shows that the organization may not have done a good job at communicating the process, strategies, or vision throughout the organization. It could also be that the organization might have some policies, procedures, or custom that may not have been embedded in the way it operates. For example, Table 12-2 shows that even though the employee considers labor law and employment protection as an important issue, he or she does not see the company being compliant. While quadrant II shows the drivers that are important but invisible, quadrant III shows the forces that may not be considered important for the organization but are visible its environment. The organization will need to consider this quadrant very thoughtfully, primarily because it might be practicing some policies and procedures and encouraging certain behavior that does not contribute to its performance. Moreover, it may even be spending money on some type of a training program, technological equipment, or promotional events that may not be effectively serving their intended purpose. Quadrant IV displays the forces or drivers that are neither important nor visible. Apparently it seems to be a less concerning quadrant for the organization to consider.

However, since the employees identified all the driving forces to be important in the first stage, anything identified as "not important" and "not visible" may be concerning. This quadrant could indicate that an employee may not have been able to comprehend the significance of a certain driving force. Alternately, the leadership may not have been able to communicate effectively to demonstrate the significance of a driving force. In any case, the organization should be able to determine, based on its own strategic position, how to evaluate the drivers placed in quadrant IV. A good example could be the fact in Table 12-3, quadrant IV, the participant does not consider minority opinion to be an important and visible issue. It has been a proven fact that often times the minority opinion might help the organization to survive complex situations. Moreover, it also violates a very basic notion of ethics by disregarding the rights and beliefs of some employees (Cavanagh, Moberg, & Velasquez, 1981).

Table 12-3
Presentation of the Intercultural Drivers

	I Visible		II Not Visible	
Important	**Publishing for diverse communities**	52%	Publishing for diverse communities	20%
	Capturing global customers	45%	**Capturing global customers**	49%
	Building a diverse workforce	15%	Building a diverse workforce	25%
	Respect towards other culture	55%	Respect towards other culture	25%
	Concern for minority opinion	35%	**Concern for minority opinion**	40%
Not Important	Publishing for diverse communities	17%	Publishing for diverse communities	11%
	Capturing global customers	6%	Capturing global customers	0%
	Building a diverse workforce	10%	**Building a diverse workforce**	50%
	Respect towards other culture	20%	Respect towards other culture	0%
	Concern for minority opinion	15%	Concern for minority opinion	10%
	III		IV	

As each participant places the driving forces into the position table, the next step involves examining how the participants assumed the five driving forces in the context of each of the six environmental factors. Let's assume that all of the 100 responses from ABC Publications on intercultural drivers were placed in a table (Table 12-3). The maximum percentiles have been highlighted to demonstrate in which quadrant the majority of the perceived driving forces are located. From quadrant I of Table 12-3, it appears that the majority of the participants perceive that "publishing for diverse communities" and "respect towards other culture" are important and visible intercultural drivers. However, quadrant II demonstrates that the majority of the participants contend that while they acknowledge "capturing global customers" and "concern for minority opinion" to be the important driving forces, they do not see those forces visible in the organization. Quadrant IV shows that the majority of the participants do not consider "building a diverse workforce" to be an important intercultural driver and, in fact, they also see the organization taking the similar stance. A graphical representation of the findings is shown below in Figure 12-1:

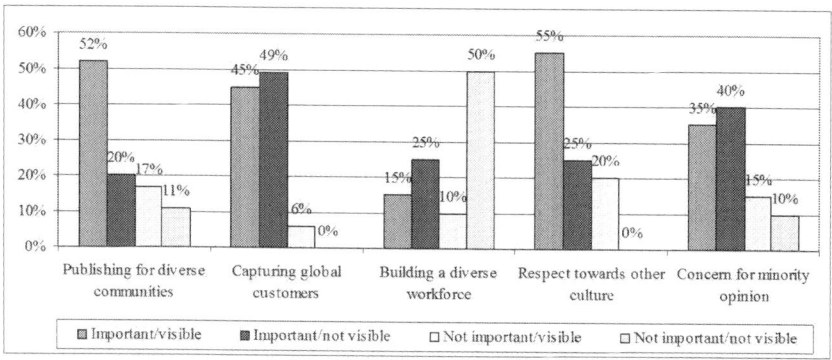

Figure 12-1. Graphical representation of the Intercultural Drivers. Columns are Important & Visible, Important & Not Visible, Not Important & Visible, Not Important & Not Visible.

As mentioned before, as an environmental scanning tool, SPELIT will help an organization to perceive where it stands in each of the environmental areas. It is assumed that any interpretation from the findings should be left to the discretion of the organizational leaders. Every organization is led by a unique leadership that is in the position to delineate how the findings would help them make a better decision under the circumstances. However, in order to facilitate the decision making by using SPELIT, another stage can be implemented to illustrate the positive and negative aspects of the driving forces. The third stage would depict the findings of the position table in a fishbone diagram (Figure 12-2).

Apparently, through the fishbone diagram, all the findings could be presented in an in-depth and objective manner. An example of the intercultural drivers has been depicted in Figure 12-2, where both negative perceptions and positive perceptions of the participants have been presented. Other environmental forces could also be presented through the fishbone diagram. Collectively, they will provide an aerial view of the positive and negative driving forces for each of the environmental factors. By looking at the depicted forces in the fishbone diagram, the leaders will not only be able to identify the positive and negative drivers, but they will also be able to differentiate the internal driving forces from the external drivers. For example, under the positive perception in Figure 12-2 "publishing for diverse communities" and "respect towards other cultures" are the drivers of internal environment because both of them are driven by internal culture. On the other hand, in the negative perception category, "capturing global customers" is not an organizations internal environmental issue. It is subject to external variables such as the nature of global market, government regulations in different countries, variations of language, and so forth. Ironically, when a negative force is identified, if the organization decides to turn that into a positive, it will have more control over the internal environment. However, when an external environmental issue is identified, the organization will have to figure out a way to adapt to the environment by making internal environmental changes.

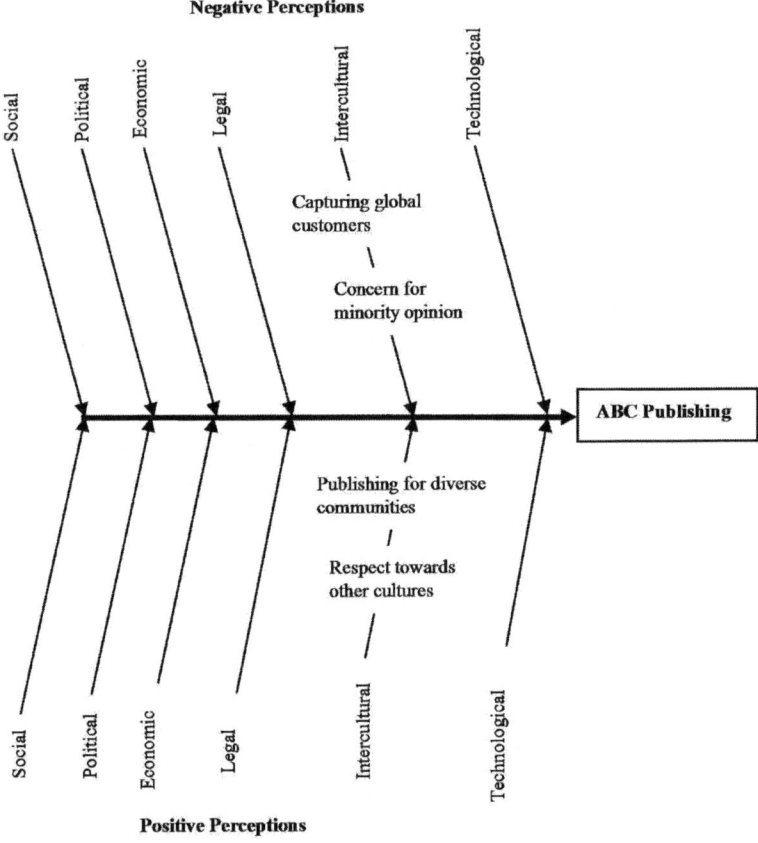

Figure 12-2. SPELIT Analysis Fishbone Diagram Showing the Findings of the Position Table.

***

Conclusion

Through the example of ABC Publications Inc., this chapter has demonstrated three major aspects: first, how SPELIT can be applied in an organization to capture different environmental drivers; second, to what extent each driver plays an important role in the organization or what essential drivers are missing from the organizational environments that may be crucial for its strategic alignment; third, how negative and positive environmental drivers could be separated. An organization could strategize to exploit the positive drivers effectively to accomplish its mission. On the other hand, it can analyze the negative forces and make appropriate schemes to deal with them. Fourth, the external and internal environments of the ABC Publications Inc. can be identified. If there is a misalignment between the external and internal environment, the management can revise its strategic direction. It is essential for an organization to be able to undertake change initiatives by adapting to the variances in the external environment as it is influenced by outside forces such as the government or industrial forces. It is also important to carry out necessary internal changes to ensure alignment between the organization's actions and its mission.

By applying SPELIT, an organization can identify where it stands. Based on this analysis, the leaders can make decisions about changing positions to align with the organizational objectives. SPELIT could be an extremely useful instrument for the consultants and practitioners that are looking for a multidimensional environmental scanning process. Finally, SPELIT could be used to identify the critical success factors for an organization. By recognizing them, the organization could initiate strategic initiatives to enhance its performance and achieve enormous growth and success.

***

References

Albright, K. S. (2004). Environmental scanning: Radar for success. *Information Management Journal, 38*(3), 38-45.

Cavanagh, G. F., Moberg, D. J., & Velasquez, M. (1981). The ethics of organizational politics. *Academy of Management. The Academy of Management Review, 6*(3), 363-374.

Keck, K. L., Leigh, T. W., & Lollar, J. G. (1995). Critical success factors in captive, multi-line insurance AG. *The Journal of Personal Selling & Sales Management, 15*(1), 17-33

Tregoe, B. B., Zimmerman, J. W., Smith, R. A., & Tobia, P. M. (1990). The driving force. *Planning Review, 18*(2), 4-16.

The SPELIT POWER MATRIX
Final Conclusions

The purpose of this text was to show how perceptive leaders can analyze environments in preparation for possible future action. We have demonstrated how methodology aligns with previous theories regarding environmental scanning and produces a workable framework for the perceptive leader. The SPELIT system looks at individual skills or the organization to analyze social, political, economic, legal, intercultural, and technological environments.

In the introduction to this text, Leo Mallette discussed Kurt Lewin's Change Theory of unfreezing, freezing, and refreezing and the necessity to analyze the situation carefully before any change. We use the best intelligence we have to analyze any situation, be it a new career, a new relationship, or a new organization before we "unfreeze" the situation. It is analogous to boarding a train and being sure that one train station is aligned with the next train station.

In the "Theoretical Foundations of SPELIT," June Schmieder-Ramirez explained the importance of the thinking that has preceded the development of the SPELIT model. She further explained that the SPELIT model can be used to assess your own strength as well as the strength of the organization. Student teachers, architect apprentices, and business leaders can all find this model useful. She further reviews the importance of "frameworks" as useful tools in any analysis and cites Graham Allison's *Essence of Decision* as an excellent text to use in organizing a political event. Another framework for analyzing organizations can be found in Bolman and Deal's *Reframing Organizations*.

She further notes the importance of a "disequilibrium causing event" that may trigger change. This disequilibrium may occur in either the "driving" or "restraining" forces that are present in any organization. Schmieder-Ramirez ends chapter one with an in-depth discussion of the definitions of each of the elements of the SPELIT model. She notes that the social part of SPELIT refers to the human interaction component of any organization and makes the assertion that learning can be a deeply social activity. She then cites how the political portion of the model concerns competing political interests, personal alignments in the organization, and competing values and assumptions. The economic portion of the model is then reviewed and is straightforward regarding the importance of financial reports and statements of economic health that are issued periodically in all organizations.

The chapter concludes with an analysis of the work concerning intercultural sensitivity and the importance of knowing the profile of employees within the organization. The technological infrastructure is also a strand that needs analysis in the organization. Without this analysis, any attempt at improving an organization from a technological state would be of little value.

Schmieder-Ramirez concludes with a reference to Clayton Christensen's analysis of the Butterfield Fabric Company that used the "driving forces" technique described in this chapter to analyze what forces would be threats versus those that would be opportunities.

Jacqueline Pritchett in her chapter on adult learning uses Knowles' theory of adult learning to explain the core principles that encourage lifelong learners. Her dialogue included is a classic example of the need to use the SPELIT model to make decisions based on a thorough analysis of the situation. One question that might be asked is: What is the most important element of the SPELIT model? You could conclude that this depends. It depends on what type of organization you are in. For example, we know that the U.S. presidency is incredibly complex and that it requires using the entire model as a tool of analysis. However, it is apparent that the political model would be very important to the president and would influence greatly his or her actions on a day-to-day basis. In contrast, the social model would be important in such human interaction businesses as counseling, teaching, and social work.

Mark Maier in chapter four visits the core assumptions of the social part of SPELIT including the human and structural frames of Bolman and Deal. He focuses on the fact that and organization's tasks must be identified, then the infrastructure should be built to help complete these tasks. He wisely notes that direction and control are not the way to motivate employees and are not the main tools of the perceptive leader. The focus in this chapter is upon relationships. Maier concludes with a fascinating analysis of those factors which inhibit the social aspects of the organization versus those factors which attend to the human factors. Maier emphasizes that we must create leverage in the organization by concentrating on purpose and vision rather than just activities. SPELIT helps us achieve our goals by ensuring that we have analyzed the organization before we seek to move it forward. Maier concludes that very few in the organization know how their activities relate to the organization as a whole. He summarizes the "can do" attitude of most great organizations with a tribute to Southwest Airlines where pilots clean up the cockpit after their flying stints.

Chapter five presents the political view of the SPELIT model. This chapter builds upon prior frameworks which include the political frame and emphasize its key importance to organizational analysis. Key strands are identified including key emerging political skills that are key to the new organizational worker.

Elizabeth Martin and Michael Lacourse discuss how economic analysis is an inherent part of the SPELIT model in chapter six. Particular economic reports are detailed in the chapter. These include the assessment of revenue sources and the assessment of expenditures. These are the two opposites and the economics environment would be a good candidate for the positive and negative effects format described in chapter 11. They conclude that the assessment of costs and expenditures is a dynamic process, where the estimated expenditures are used to determine the needed resources, while the availability of resources constraints the expenditures.

In chapter seven the legal domain of the SPELIT model is analyzed. John Tobin analyzes the root of the legal domain within an organization's environment. Tobin notes that the type of legal structure differs by country, and in a country like China the decision makers and fact finders in the legal system may be the same person. Natural Law and Legal Positivism were studied as foundations for the differing architectures of systems for enforcing law in Rule of Law systems which have evolved as the Adversarial/ Common Law system and the Inquisitorial/ Civil Law system.

Chapter eight reviews the intercultural component of SPELIT. Gale Mazur and Mike Moodian discuss the origins of intercultural communications as observed by Edward Hall and the recognition of different cultural styles of communication as emphasized by Milton Bennett and Mitch Hammer. Because of the multicultural profile of our organizations, it is important to recognize the importance of this frame in the model. The Development Model of Intercultural Sensitivity (DMIS) is described. The DMIS tests whether individuals are ethnocentric or ethnorelative. In the most sophisticated stage of ethnorelativism the individual is able to move in and out of cultures easily. As the chapter indicates, only 5% of managers are in this percentile. It is also determined that intercultural competence can be learned.

"Diffusion of innovation" is one of the topics of the technology chapter. If you do a competent technology assessment as part of this framework, you can enable CEOs and employees to make full use of technology. In chapter nine, Maurice Shihadi details how a technology audit can be made part of the SPELIT model.

Some of the environments that may need to be studied in specialized circumstances or in some organizations are discussed by Leo Mallette in chapter ten.

The last two chapters presented short vignettes and examples of the SPELIT analysis method (chapter eleven) and a detailed, report-length, SPELIT analysis of a publishing organization (chapter twelve).

In conclusion, the chapters presented each strand of the SPELIT POWER MATRIX and indicated how this scanning model can aid in the assessment of the organization. The perceptive leader can take this model and use it as a tool for scanning the organization.

Made in the USA
Lexington, KY
17 April 2015